Start To Finish:
A Life Well-Lived

The Choices and Forces
That Shape It

Robert W Lutz

Dedication

To my grandchildren, Leila and Kent.

Acknowledgment

I want to thank my editorial team for all their help and encouragement in bringing this book to publication. In particular, I need to thank Bob Collins and Madison Cooper who oversaw and coordinated this entire endeavor, and provided me with much needed guidance throughout.

This book draws heavily on the research and reviews of investigators studying the cornerstones of what makes us healthy and what makes life satisfying and meaningful. The research and reviews of Drs. Roy Baumeister, Ed Diener, David Myers, and Martin Seligman, in particular, provided me with insights on what leads to a good, full life. The research of Dr. John Gottman deepened my understanding of communication styles among couples. And the landmark review of usual vs. successful aging by Drs. John Rowe and Robert Kahn gave me insight into the great variability in how people age, and the powerful influence of lifestyle. I owe thanks to them all and many others.

About the Author

Robert Lutz worked nights on the waterfront as a longshoreman for twenty years while completing college, internship, fellowships, and even during his first year on faculty at UCSF Medical Center. He sometimes joked that he was "Dr. Lutz" in the daytime and "Hey You" at night.

Lutz's career in psychology focused on Behavioral Medicine and Cognitive-Behavioral interventions. While on faculty in the Departments of Medicine and Anesthesia at UCSF Medical Center, he developed and directed the Behavioral Program for their Multidisciplinary Pain Management Center. He then transitioned his career to a combination of teaching and private practice. He retired as a tenured professor in 2017.

Now, he spends many of his days hiking the hills North of San Francisco, where he lives. He has long been an avid reader of anything to do with evolution and human evolution in particular. His life experience and deep appreciation for our shared human characteristics and challenges are reflected in this book.

Table of Contents

Introduction

Have you ever sensed something or had an immediate feeling about someone and didn't know why? Of course, you did. We all evolved together as homo sapiens and share much in terms of our perceptual abilities. Limbic system structures in our middle brain, the diencephalon, are the seat of our emotions. Stimuli are detected and processed independently by the limbic system outside our awareness, and responded to by giving us feelings that then influence our conscious attention and actions.

I discuss in Chapter Two that limbic system processing underlies what we commonly refer to as intuition or gut feelings. So, what stimuli are processed and responded to outside our awareness? The easy answer is that limbic system structures are simply processing and responding to the same range of stimuli that we might consciously perceive, but processing it independently and outside our awareness. I'm sure that is sometimes the all of it. I don't believe it is always the all of it though.

There is so much we don't yet fully understand… how the brain creates consciousness, or even how best to define consciousness. And what of the stimuli we're responding to outside consciousness? Is it limited to sounds, sights and smells that we can otherwise perceive? I don't believe so. Pheromones? Certainly, a maybe. Something akin to telepathy? That's a maybe too.

I remember sitting at my kitchen table alone at home one day, grading term papers as I recall. But I had the strangest feeling I was being watched. Impossible I thought. Yet, I couldn't shake the feeling. Then I looked up through the skylight above my kitchen table, and there was a Blue Jay with its head cocked starring down at me. A Blue Jay! Coincidence? Maybe, but I have my doubts.

I've had other experiences where I recognized someone from a distance walking away with their back to me. Then, they suddenly stopped, turned around, saw me, we made eye contact and both waved. How did that and similar other occurrences happen? Coincidence again? I don't believe so. There is so much we don't know, and it is part of what makes life and science exciting. There is always more to know.

I have tried in this book to address a few of the forces and challenges that are common to us all. Can't imagine there is anyone who doesn't want what can be honestly described as a full, good life. Or, who wouldn't choose health and vigor, over illness and fatigue. While many questions remain unanswered, there are at least many significant influences for how life unfolds that we understand well-enough to make meaningful predictions. More importantly perhaps, enough concrete knowledge for individuals to make choices and build habits that stack the odds in their favor for a good, full and long life. I have tried to reveal and explain some of those forces and choices in this book, and hope that you find them helpful.

Chapter 1
Choices and Forces

For most of human history, we lived as hunter-gatherers, and life's demands changed little from generation to generation. We lived in small, cohesive groups, sustaining ourselves by hunting animals and gathering edible plants. Challenges were predictable, and expectations were straightforward. It was the several million years of evolution in those ancestral environments that shaped our core needs and motivations. Even though the world looks very different now, those core human needs are still with us - and they still play a big role in what makes life feel full and meaningful today.

Think about how books and stories can touch people all over the world. They go beyond language, culture, and even time. Thoughts, feelings, and motives expressed in classic literature written two thousand years ago are still completely recognizable. Smiles, snarls, and other basic emotional expressions are understood universally. In culture, language, lifestyle, diet, technology, and religious beliefs, we are undeniably diverse. Yet, when we look at the basics, those disparities melt away.

Whether modern or Stone Age, Western or Eastern, rich or poor, the specific things people want to have, become, achieve, and do are dramatically variable. But not the underlying motivations. The life of a CEO may seem worlds apart from that of a hunter-gatherer, yet behind all the surface differences are two people motivated to display their competence, make their way in the world, and gain social acceptance and recognition. Our basic drives and needs haven't really changed.

Is there any culture where people wouldn't

choose a life filled with a sense of belonging and caring over one marked by alienation? Who doesn't want to feel respected, comfortable, and secure? Is there anyone who doesn't want the freedom to pursue joy, pleasure, and a sense of meaning? The inevitable ups and downs of life aside, who doesn't want a life that can honestly be described as good and full? The pursuit of happiness is a universal motivation.

Meeting Human Needs

Like all living beings, we need to meet a range of needs in order to thrive. True human needs, however, are distinct from individual needs and wants. These basic needs are part of being human and can be seen in people across all populations and cultures. For example, an individual working in technology may genuinely need their computer and cell phone to fulfill their work and social roles. And there is an endless list of things people may simply want. However, personal needs and wants like these are not the same as those that qualify as human needs.

Human needs manifest across populations, and whether these needs are met or not have clear effects on a person's physical and mental health. Basic biological needs, such as food and water, clearly meet these criteria. The longer we're deprived of either, the more consumed we become with obtaining them. And obtain them we must, in order to survive.

The consequences of unmet social and emotional needs are also demonstrable, though they tend to emerge over a longer time span. We evolved as social beings. Holding and nurturing infants and children has been shown to significantly improve our psychological and neurological development, as well as our chances of survival. Examination of records and of the children raised in orphanages during wartime, where food was available, but human nurturance was absent, revealed grossly abnormal physical and psychological development, along with alarmingly high mortality rates. Human touch and nurturance are not luxuries, but necessities.

As adults, regular, positive, and ongoing contact with people we care about and who care about us in return has been found to be the strongest predictor of life satisfaction. In contrast, isolation and alienation take a measurable toll on our overall well-being. Research shows that regular contact within close, caring relationships is a human need. When our social and emotional needs aren't met over a long period, it takes a toll on both our mental and physical health.

As unromantic as it may sound, romantic relationships are not necessary to fulfill our social needs. Not all romantic partnerships are happy or successful, and unhappy marriages tend to actually reduce life satisfaction and health. However, when a person is in a positive romantic relationship, it is, in itself, predictive of higher life satisfaction and better long-term health. We can absolutely fulfill our social needs and lead a wonderfully happy life without a romantic attachment, but when a successful romantic partnership is also present, it's the icing on the cake.

Besides our social needs, having meaningful goals and leisure activities to enjoy also plays a big role in feeling satisfied with life. Living a fulfilling life means staying involved in things that matter to us. Activities like watching TV can be a pleasurable compliment to active and meaningful engagement in life for some people, but not a substitute. People who participate in more active and engaging uses of their time report significantly higher life satisfaction than those who do not.

Enjoying active hobbies that get us moving also helps lay the groundwork for staying physically healthy. In fact, leisure-time physical activity levels are strongly predictive of long-term health. A young person who develops healthy relationships and leisure outlets and also finds a satisfying, viable way to make a living is well on their way to a full and satisfying life. It's no guarantee, but it's a highly encouraging start!

Money and Life Satisfaction

Both common observation and a substantial body of research confirm that wealth, or fame, is neither a requirement nor a guarantee of personal happiness. That's not to say money doesn't matter. Studies consistently show that lacking sufficient income to reliably meet basic living expenses is linked to higher stress, a reduced sense of control, poorer health, and lower life satisfaction. Clearly, making our way in the world successfully enough to meet the practical demands of life is important.

However, the same line of research also reveals that once income reaches a level sufficient to meet those basic needs, further increases have a surprisingly negligible impact on life satisfaction. Someone may be able to buy their way out of hardship, but they don't have to be rich to afford a good, full life.

To be clear, there is nothing bad about being wealthy. Wealth provides a myriad of advantages and options. However, it doesn't negate or replace the importance of other factors, like close relationships and a sense of accomplishment, that give life meaning and satisfaction. And while fame and fortune are achieved by relatively few, the core ingredients of a good, full life are widely attainable.

Health and Life Satisfaction

The relationship between health and life satisfaction is a bit like money and happiness. As with poverty, chronic poor health, or losing the ability to do the things we enjoy, can significantly lower life satisfaction. But just as wealth doesn't guarantee happiness, neither does good health.

Most people in the general population are not

facing an immediate medical crisis, and good health is easily taken for granted. Take vision, for example. Chances are you have adequate eyesight, even if it requires correction with glasses or contact lenses. Now, imagine suddenly losing your vision - you would understandably feel distressed. If you later regained your vision, you'd likely feel elated.

Yet, for those of us who can see, we wake up every day without giving it a second thought. We don't exclaim, "This is wonderful. I can see!" Our emotions are largely tied to change. When health problems arise, they can lower our sense of well-being. But when our health is stable or good, it usually goes unnoticed.

A great deal of research has identified additional factors and personal characteristics that are predictive of a happy and fulfilling life. Personal characteristics such as extraversion, a positive or optimistic outlook, and the absence of significant mental health issues are also associated with higher life satisfaction. While genetics play a role in shaping all of our personal traits, each of these factors can also be influenced by conscious effort and lifestyle choices. Strategies for managing stress and developing a more positive thinking style and communicating effectively will be discussed in further chapters.

Are there exceptions? Of course. Research on life satisfaction doesn't describe every individual's experience but rather what tends to be true for the sampled groups on average. Knowing which factors usually lead to desirable outcomes helps us make smarter, more informed choices. The existence of exceptions - or the fact that a finding represents just one part of a larger puzzle - doesn't invalidate the research. Think of research as a way to clarify how things usually work and fit together. That's enough to make research findings useful for improving our own decision-making and, in turn, increasing our personal odds of success. Just as not smoking improves our chances of staying healthy, there are many steps we can take to improve our odds of achieving a happy and meaningful life.

Two Dimensions of a Good, Full Life

Knowledge is power. All the things that affect how happy and well we feel come from a mix and balance of two basic tracks in life. Regardless of culture or lifestyle, a good life depends on both taking care of business and enjoying the journey.

They are the yin and yang of a good, full life. Focusing on only one doesn't cut it.

Most of us have probably met people who put a great deal of energy into work and getting ahead, but don't really know how to relax and enjoy life. That kind of imbalance backfires. Someone might be highly successful in earning a living, but we wouldn't describe their life as good and full if they were also chronically stressed or unloved. On the other hand, we've also likely met people who know how to relax and enjoy themselves - they might even be the life of the party. But if they regularly fail to plan ahead and take care of business, that also backfires. It takes both, and staying mindful of that balance can be helpful.

Like all living organisms, we need to find a way to make our way in the world. When someone is "taking care of business," they're doing just that – making their way in the world successfully. They're being mindful and putting in the effort to meet both their current needs and future goals. In the past, planning for the future might have just meant storing enough food to last through the winter. Today, it usually includes things like career planning, saving for retirement, and taking care of our long-term health. Whether it comes easily or not, taking care of both the present and the future is a basic part of living a good, fulfilling life, and it always has been.

But to really have a good and full life, we also need to enjoy the journey. That means meeting our social and emotional needs, too. To fully enjoy life, we need close, meaningful relationships and ways to spend our time that we find gratifying -activities that give us a sense of meaning, purpose, pride, or simple enjoyment. While we can survive without caring relationships or while stuck in a dead-end job, we wouldn't describe that life as good and full.

Of course, some endeavors fulfill both sides of the equation. Work and the relationships we form through it can be a deep source of meaning and satisfaction. Taking care of our long-term health can include enjoying delicious, healthy meals and getting exercise through activities we genuinely enjoy. But of course, taking care of business and enjoying ourselves don't always go hand in hand. Some food and lifestyle choices that bring immediate gratification may be unhealthy and undermine our long-term goals. And some jobs are just a paycheck, perhaps even a meager one.

There are many factors that help or hinder our

ability to achieve a good life, some within our control and some not. Much will be said in the next chapter about why self-defeating behavior is so common and how we can stack the odds in our favor as we pursue both individual success and the shared goal of a good life. Still, it would be irresponsible not to first acknowledge that the playing field is far from level.

The Fundamental Role of Luck

While personal effort clearly plays a role in who does well in life, it never operates alone. Factors outside our control (pure luck) permeate our lives in ways that easily go unappreciated. We don't get to choose our genetic makeup, the family circumstances we're born into, the society we grow up in, or the time period in which we live. Yet these factors have a major influence on the course our lives take. Yes, we can take credit for our choices, hard work, and how well we use our natural abilities, but we can never take all the credit. It's always a complex interaction of factors, and pure luck plays a huge and fundamental role.

A widely accepted axiom about what makes us all who we are is the interaction between nature and nurture. Nature refers to our genetic blueprint for development - our inherited potential. Our genetic makeup strongly influences our physical traits and capabilities, our intelligence and creativity, our risks for mental and physical health issues, and our personality traits. And none of that is up to us. This genetic variability means some things are easier for some, harder for others, or simply out of reach. The best schooling can't turn the average person into an Einstein, just as the best training can't turn just anyone into a Michael

Jordan. Even getting into certain competitive fields often requires mental or physical abilities far above average, and that alone disqualifies a whole lot of people.

Nurture encompasses the entirety of our life experiences and environment, from the womb to the grave. Even here, especially in childhood, much of what shapes us lies outside our control. Some children grow up with the support and encouragement they need to succeed in school and in life. Others with similar needs aren't so lucky.

Much of the critical information we learn growing up about what matters and how to live our lives comes from our own experiences and what we observe around us. If an average child is lucky enough to be born into a loving, stable family in a place where good role models and opportunities for growth are easy to find, it's a major advantage in life. It's no guarantee of success, but it certainly sets the stage for a successful life.

Now contrast that with children born into social environments lacking stability and positive role modeling. Sure, people can learn to do things differently and better than how they were treated or what they saw modeled around them. Given access to opportunity, which is not guaranteed, some will beat the odds. But it's a much harder and more precarious path. And, of course, most people don't overcome severe odds. A child growing up in a severely impoverished environment may not even know that better options exist. A nurturing environment can help someone reach their potential, while a grossly inadequate or restrictive environment can act like a sledgehammer and crush potential.

Controlling What We Can

The interaction of nature and nurture is complex and ongoing throughout our lives. While many powerful influences lie beyond our control, there are still numerous factors we can control - and must, if we want to improve our odds of living a good, full life. We may inherit a particular genetic makeup, but whether and how those genes are expressed often depends on our environment and the choices we make. Through the decisions we make, we can shape, modify, or even limit the influence of certain genetically based traits.

Take, for example, two people whose genetic makeup makes them especially vulnerable to the toxins in cigarette smoke. Due to inherited factors, likely unknown to them, they are more likely to suffer serious health consequences from smoking than the average person. However, if their environments differ such that one takes up smoking and the other adopts a healthier lifestyle, their long-term health outcomes will diverge dramatically despite their similar genetic risks. That's why it's often said: *Nature loads the gun, but lifestyle pulls the trigger... or not!*

Our genetic makeup also influences our choices and experiences in life. For instance, take two people who both give sports or music a serious try in school. Because of genetically influenced differences in physical ability or musical aptitude, one may find it easier to excel than the other. How good we are at something often affects how much we enjoy it and how motivated we are to keep going. If someone really gets into playing music, for example, it can influence who they meet and the relationships they build along the way.

We all have strengths and weaknesses, which means certain things come more easily or are more difficult to some than to others. And that applies across the board: from managing emotions, to losing weight, to impulse control, to staying healthy, and just about any personal variable you care to measure. That same mix of strengths and weaknesses also shows up in our natural talents and abilities, making some activities simple for some people while others may need more time and effort to succeed. Some pursuits, especially those that demand rare abilities or access to opportunities, may even be entirely closed off to all but a select few.

For example, if you want to play professional

basketball in the NBA, you need to have the opportunity to learn and play the game, possess exceptional athletic talent, be passionate about the sport, receive good coaching, and get noticed by the right people. Oh, and it helps to be especially tall, too! That's a lot of 'ands.' Needless to say, extremely few people check all those boxes. Fortunately, while some goals and careers do require special abilities or characteristics, most do not.

The Bell-Shaped Curve

Take a look at the distribution of almost any human trait across the general population. It usually forms a bell-shaped curve, with most people clustered around the middle and fewer people at either extreme. This "bell-shaped curve," also known as a normal distribution, tells us that most people fall within the average range for any given trait - whether it's shoe size, IQ, or something else. Being average is good enough for the vast majority of human endeavors, provided it's paired with effort and opportunity. It's certainly adequate if the goal is simply to lead a good, full life.

With enough commitment, it often doesn't matter if something takes one person longer to learn or master than it does another. Once they've got it, they've got it. At that point, other factors, like interest, opportunity, and work ethic, begin to shape long-term success in a chosen path or career. After all, you don't have to perform at an elite or professional level to be competent or to enjoy something. Even when a particular career path or goal is out of reach due to someone's makeup or abilities, it usually doesn't matter much as long as other good options exist.

Finding Good Matches

In general, people tend to gravitate toward where their interests, abilities, and opportunities align, choosing the best available option. One major benefit of a college education beyond the knowledge gained is that it opens up more options, and in many cases, it's a prerequisite for certain careers. But for many, the essential task is simply to find a suitable match for our individual interests and abilities. That's a much more doable task than having to land a particular job or career. The same principle applies to our social success, too.

The notion that 'opposites attract' is largely a myth. Research shows that people are drawn to those who are similar to themselves. While there may be exceptions, rare cases where true opposites come together, it's far from the norm. The myth is generally bolstered by a bias in observation. For example, two people might share a similar background in terms of culture, race, religion, socioeconomic status, age, and physical attractiveness. But if one is extremely shy and quiet while the other is very outgoing, observers may fixate on that difference and conclude, "See, opposites attract," while overlooking all the ways they're alike.

Ultimately, we're all just looking for work, friendships, romantic partners, and a lifestyle that feels like a good fit. And in a large society, there are (theoretically, at least) many potential matches out there for everyone. A good, full life is well within reach - *provided* opportunity exists.

On a personal level, success in life hinges

heavily on how well we manage the factors within our control that affect our chances for that good, full life. And if we're fortunate enough to have the freedom and opportunity to make meaningful choices, we can stack the odds in our favor. It's not a guarantee; there are always exceptions, but the 'rule' is what allows us to put the odds in our favor.

Track yourself into a job that suits you and provides a decent income, and you may still face financial hardship or job dissatisfaction, but far less often. Exercise regularly, eat well, and avoid substance abuse, and you may still develop serious health problems. But on average, you'll do so much less frequently and at a later age than someone who doesn't follow a healthy lifestyle. And if you treat others the way you'd like to be treated, you're more likely to build stronger, more stable relationships.

It's all about the odds. But it's not a level playing field.

Luck plays a major role in the course of our lives. Some people are born with exceptional natural abilities, access to opportunities, strong support systems, and even second chances - advantages others never get. And for some, factors like environmental disasters, personal trauma, or systemic oppression can leave no real chance at all.

It's impossible to completely eliminate the fundamental role that luck plays in how life unfolds. Nonetheless, societies can prioritize policies that help level the playing field. Greater government support for quality child care, preschools, school resource specialists, and nutritional programs—especially for schools and low-income families—along with living wages and affordable health care for all, would be a strong and much-needed step forward.

Chapter 2
Stress and Emotions

Have you ever sensed something was wrong, but couldn't say why? What we commonly call 'intuition' or a 'gut feeling' is actually our brain's limbic system at work that processes things without us even realizing it. Cues are detected without our conscious knowledge, triggering an emotion-based reaction via limbic system structures in the middle brain (diencephalon). We sense something but may not know why. This kind of reaction can be helpful, like steering us away from danger or helping us make quick decisions. But it's no guarantee that our emotion-based reactions are always leading us in the right or desired direction.

The limbic system and the feelings it creates show up in our lives in many ways. For example, making good choices or reaching our goals often means we have to delay gratification, and that's not always easy. Our long-term goals can clash with what we want right now. If you've ever tried to lose weight, you've no doubt experienced the struggle between your emotional brain and higher intellectual processes. Your rational mind may say, "I want to lose weight; therefore, I will eat healthier choices and smaller portions." Ah, if only it were that easy. Unfortunately, your limbic system may be signaling, all too clearly in the moment, that you're really hungry and in the mood for pizza, not vegetables.

That's also why it's possible to meet someone who seems to have all the qualities we thought we were looking for in a romantic partner, but still not feel attracted to them. Limbic system processing has its own input and conclusions. Or, as this was noted long ago: "The heart has its own reasons, which reason does not know" (Pascal, 1670).

A Tiny Bit of Brain Anatomy and Function

The middle part of the brain, called the diencephalon, sits right on top of the brain stem and is surrounded by the brain's outer layer, known as the cerebral cortex. While humans don't have the biggest brains, we do have large brains for our body size, especially when it comes to the cerebral cortex. This area is where conscious thinking, planning, and problem-solving happen, and we have more of it (proportionally) than other species.

The middle brain can be thought of as a mammalian adaptation, as it is greatly enlarged in mammals. These enhanced structures give mammals a much wider range of information processing and response options compared to species such as fish and reptiles. This region of the brain includes the hypothalamus, amygdala, hippocampus, and cingulate gyrus - limbic system structures that are the seat of our emotions. These structures create feeling states such as hunger, thirst, fear, and anger - all of them. And they influence us.

Attention, motivation, body responses, and emotions are all deeply connected. We cannot get stressed, for example, without the body preparing for action. And that's true whether action is actually called for or not. So, if we get angry or anxious at someone tailgating us, even when we're keeping up just fine with the traffic in our lane, our bodies react, whether we are aware of it or not. Muscles tense a bit, our blood pressure rises, blood sugar levels increase to provide active energy, and our attention becomes focused on the perceived threat and how best to respond. All this, even though we're just sitting in our car driving safely.

Stress reactions are a primitive response to perceived threats that are not unique to humans. This basic response pattern improves survival rates by preparing us to better run or fight. That's why it is commonly referred to as the fight-or-flight response. Unfortunately, modern life presents stress in forms we can't run from or physically fight, like work deadlines, financial worries, or traffic. And these ongoing stressors can affect both our physical and mental health.

Hans Selye (1956, 1976) did pioneering research linking stress to health. Some of his studies involved stressing rats non-stop without physically harming them, at least not directly. Despite having adequate food and water, rats died under prolonged stress. The idea that prolonged stress might not only exhaust us but also eventually kill us got a lot of attention. There's no shortage of people who feel chronically stressed. Selye's data suggested a dire prediction. Fortunately, there are important differences between Selye's lab animals and our experience of stress.

Unlike rats in a cage, humans under stress usually get breaks - we have downtime and vacations from most sources of stress. That makes a difference. People also have the ability to learn new coping skills or change difficult situations, which rats stuck in a cage do not. Even if someone is trapped in a truly stressful situation and reaches the stage of exhaustion, they would typically receive care and perhaps even forced downtime in the form of disability leave. Most importantly, we now know that our energy to cope isn't limited. Unlike what researchers first believed, we can bounce back and renew our energy and coping reserves. People can feel completely beaten down and still recover, sometimes coming back stronger than before.

Defining 'Stress-Related' Health Problems

Many stress-related health problems stem from chronic (long-term) stress. With chronic stress, the body is not only being taxed and compromised for a long time, but it's also not getting enough time to rest and recover. Chronic stress also has the ability to compromise our immune system, which is something that acute stress typically does not do in healthy individuals. With chronic stress, the wear and tear caused by physical and behavioral changes can accumulate and worsen over time.

For people with existing stress-related problems and vulnerabilities, even a single day of high-stress can aggravate symptoms. And if a stressor is severe enough and traumatizing, it can trigger an anxiety disorder in even perfectly healthy individuals.

'Hypochondriac' is a term that refers to people who believe they are sick when they are not. That is not what 'stress-related' means. Calling a health problem 'stress-related' should not be construed as meaning that the problem isn't real or is 'just in someone's head.' Stress produces real, measurable changes in the body that can initiate or aggravate legitimate medical conditions. In their critical review, Pelletier and Lutz (1988) note that stress has been determined to be a major factor in a wide range of conditions. These include heart disease, high blood pressure, gastro-intestinal problems, pain disorders, skin issues, and a higher risk of infections like colds and flu. They also note that stress has been shown to affect health related behaviors such as smoking and alcohol use, as well as mental health more generally.

To say that a particular health problem is 'stress-related' simply means that stress plays a role in initiating or worsening the condition. Stress does not have to be the direct or sole cause of a health problem for it to qualify as stress-related. For example, a person may have neck pain stemming directly from an auto accident, yet that pain may later be classified as stress-related if stress aggravates it, as it likely could. Many biological changes occur in times of stress, along with potential changes in health-related behaviors. It is these physiological and behavioral changes that link stress and health.

Let's see how this works.

Physiological and Behavioral Changes Link Stress to Health

Stress can influence health through two primary pathways:

1. Physiological changes associated with the stress response.

2. Behavioral changes that commonly occur under stress.

The table below outlines examples of each pathway. For instance, consider gastrointestinal issues such as heartburn, ulcers, and irritable bowel syndrome. Why are these problems aggravated by stress? It's because stress disrupts normal digestive processes and blood flow patterns (physiological changes) and may also influence the quantity and quality of the food choices we make (behavioral changes). Various stress-related health problems can be attributed to one or both of these pathways.

Two Pathways to Stress-Related Health Problems

PATHWAY ONE
Physiological Changes That Can Cause or Aggravate Health Problems

01 Increased workload on the heart

02 Elevated blood pressure

03 Increased spasms and wear on arterial walls

04 Increased circulating blood sugar levels and blood viscosity (thickness)

05 Elevated cholesterol levels

06 Increased muscle tension

07 Altered blood flow patterns

08 Disruption of digestive processes

09 Compromised immune function under chronic stress

10 Inhibition of the inflammatory response

PATHWAY TWO
Behavioral Changes That Can Cause or Aggravate Health Problems

01 Diet: Poorer food choices (quantity and quality) may occur as people seek quick, easy options.

02 Exercise: People may exercise less than they otherwise would if they feel tired or beaten down at the end of a stressful day.

03 Smoking: People who smoke may smoke more under stress.

04 Substance Use: Increased use of alcohol, drugs, or caffeine as a form of escape or self-medication.

05 Accident-Prone Behavior: Attentiveness to tasks at hand may decrease when someone is focused on sources of stress. Aggressive behaviors can also increase. These changes can lead not only to more driving accidents but also to other types of accidents and altercations.

06 Sleep Deprivation: Stress can cause insomnia or prompt people to reduce sleep in order to "get more done."

Of course, behaviors don't have to change in a negative direction during times of stress. Some people exercise more and eat healthier when stressed because they know it helps reduce stress and ward off stress-related problems. Unfortunately, this proactive response is the exception rather than the rule. At the end of a stressful day, far more people opt for grabbing something to eat that is quick and easy (which usually equates to less healthy choices), just like people who smoke tend to smoke more cigarettes during times of stress, not less.

Stress and Mental Health

Stress affects our mental health in much the same way it impacts our physical well-being. It can trigger the onset of mental health conditions, especially anxiety and depression, and can also worsen pre-existing mental health problems, whether the stress is acute or chronic. Additionally, the link between stress and mental health is often a two-way street. Our perception of stressors varies from person to person. For instance, being asked to speak briefly at an event might feel like an exciting opportunity to one person but provoke intense anxiety in another. Individuals who are anxiety-prone, anger-prone, or depression-prone, as well as those with low self-esteem, often perceive situations and demands as more stressful than those without such susceptibilities. Subsequent chapters will explore how our thinking and communication styles can influence our stress levels, as well as examine mental health and its treatments.

Positive Stress

Stress is usually thought of in negative terms, as reflected in expressions like "I'm under so much stress" or "I feel so stressed." However, stress often occurs in ways that can enhance our performance or enjoyment. Not all stress is bad.

People watch scary movies or ride roller coasters in part for the excitement and adrenaline rush brought on by such mildly stressful activities. In many cases, the increased energy, focus, and emotional reactivity add to the enjoyment of the experience. After all, if a horror movie isn't at least a little scary, it can feel like a letdown.

In some situations, moderate stress adds to the fun of what we're doing. Other times, stress may not contribute to enjoyment but instead helps improve performance. Consider the stress-related burst of energy, focus, and motivation a student might experience before an exam. A chapter that seemed too dry to read carefully a few weeks earlier is suddenly reviewed in detail as the test date approaches and as their stress level rises accordingly. Stress can be positive when it helps us perform better, even if the feeling itself isn't pleasant. In fact, that is often the case.

Stress and Performance

Yerkes and Dodson (1908) were the psychologists who introduced the concept more than one hundred years ago that the relationship between stress (or what they termed arousal) and performance follows an inverted-U shape. Since then, considerable research has supported the basic premise that too little or too much arousal (stress) is detrimental to performance.

For instance, if you had a shoulder-wide plank lying on the floor, most people would be able and willing to walk across it for forty feet if there were a reason to do so. In fact, it's such an easy task that many could practically do it blindfolded. Now, imagine extending that same plank between two tall buildings, with no wind or bounce in the plank.

Technically, it's still the same task. However, the perceived danger of falling to one's death will introduce a powerful dose of stress to most people. At this point, the stress level would be so high for many people that few would even attempt to walk it, no matter how big the reward. And if everyone were forced to try, we could easily imagine some failing. With enough stress, people may lose coordination or even become faint. This shows how too much stress, even in a physically simple activity, can interfere with performance.

Recent research has shown that the amount of arousal that becomes too much for optimal performance depends on the type of task, the performer's ability, and whether the physical arousal is accompanied by high anxiety. Imagine rating stress on a scale from zero to ten, with zero being no stress and ten being extreme stress. If

48

you're trying to learn and perform a complex sequence of movements, a stress level of six might be too high and push you outside the optimal zone. On the other hand, if you're running your fastest in a one-mile race, a level six might be right in the optimal zone. While the ideal level of arousal for various tasks may change, the basic relationship between arousal and performance described by Yerkes and Dodson remains the same.

Stress levels within the optimal zone, not too high or too low, enhance performance. This understanding has practical implications. Consider a student who experiences test anxiety. If they delay studying until the night before the exam, their stress may spike too high to allow for effective focus or memory retention. All students, but especially those prone to test anxiety, can benefit from beginning their study process earlier, before their stress level potentially exceeds the optimal zone. This principle applies to many other real-life situations. If you're putting off a task that ultimately has to be done because even thinking about it makes you anxious, that anxiety will likely intensify as the deadline approaches.

The idea of an optimal arousal zone also applies more broadly to life. Without enough challenge and stimulation, life can become dull. Although challenges can be stressful, meeting them is a vital part of personal growth and achievement. On the other hand, when challenges and stimulation exceed a person's coping resources, they can become overwhelming and distressing. The key is to find a balance. Challenges and stimulation that are sufficient but not excessive keep life engaging and promote growth.

In moderation, stress can be beneficial and add zest to life.

Managing Our Emotions

The fact that the midbrain structures and limbic system processes are not under direct conscious control is why you can't simply tell yourself not to be afraid, angry, or jealous. We can't just turn our emotions and stress responses on and off like we can consciously move our fingers. For example, a person with an extreme fear of heights may logically know, with complete certainty, that a footbridge is safe, yet still struggle to control the fear they feel when trying to cross it.

New responses, however, can be learned. Returning to the example of irrational fear, people can become less reactive through repeated, incremental, and non-harmful exposure to the feared situation. In fact, *graduated exposure* leading to *habituation* (desensitization) is one of the most effective tools cognitive-behavioral therapists use to help individuals overcome specific phobias. Some excessive or irrational fears have no clear cause and seem to be part of natural genetic diversity. However, other fears can be traced back to specific experiences and reflect what's known as a classically conditioned response.

Classical conditioning is a type of learning where involuntary reactions, like emotions, become linked to certain environmental triggers or cues. The structures of the midbrain and limbic system play a central role in this type of learning and reactivity. Imagine one of our ancestors smelled something unusual, ignored it, and then narrowly escaped a predator moments later. That particular smell would likely become associated with danger and would not be ignored the next time.

While such deep-seated learning can sometimes be protective or even life-saving, it can also be faulty. A person may learn to fear or mistrust something that is completely harmless. There's an experiment that shows how this happens. A young boy was playing with a small, furry animal that he liked. Then, he was scared from behind while playing. After a few more times of this happening, the boy became conditioned to feel scared of the small animal and would scream and cry when it was brought near. It must be noted that ethics and safeguards in research have thankfully improved significantly since that study was done, and that study would not be allowed to run now!

Because emotions are closely tied to our motivations, the associations we make can have strong and lasting impacts. For example, teaching a child a new skill while keeping the experience fun and relaxed can help the child feel positive about learning in the future. Beyond simply acquiring the skill, the child may, through classical conditioning, develop a general sense of enjoyment or confidence toward new learning tasks. In contrast, a young child who is yelled at or rejected for making mistakes will have a very different learning experience. That child may develop fear or other negative emotions as a classically conditioned response to similar tasks in the future.

Fortunately, faulty learning can be unlearned. With conscious effort, we can develop new, more adaptive responses to old emotional triggers. The forthcoming chapters offer insights and "how-to" information for managing our emotions through positive thinking and effective communication.

Self-Defeating Behavior

Self-defeating behaviors are those that satisfy a short-term desire or reward at the expense of more important long-term goals. Immediate rewards are hard to resist and underlie both addictive behavior and self-defeating behavior more generally.

Let's use quitting smoking as an example. Imagine someone who has been smoking two packs a day for many years and then has a mild heart attack. Their physician tells them bluntly that if they don't want to have another heart attack that will likely be more severe, they need to stop smoking. The person is scared, doesn't want to die, and fully believes what the doctor says. You might think that would be enough, and they would never smoke again. But of course, some people truly want to quit and still aren't able to.

While the long-term benefits of quitting are obvious and enormous, we can easily imagine someone, in a particularly stressful moment, giving in to their nicotine cravings. Perhaps they tell themselves it's just this once and not a big deal. Giving in brings immediate relief by satisfying the craving. Then one cigarette leads to another, and another. There are endless examples of this kind of self-defeating behavior, where someone satisfies an immediate desire at the expense of a more important goal. Actions that are immediately pleasurable or reduce distress are hard to resist. Yet, the ability to delay gratification *when needed* so as to move our life goals forward is essential for our long-term well-being.

Fortunately, there are ways to make life's challenges less difficult and less stressful. Knowing what we want, how to get what we want, and how to stay motivated are key and demand self-awareness.

Self-Awareness and Emotional Intelligence

"Know thyself" is age-old advice. The importance of understanding both ourselves and other people—their feelings, motives, and intentions—has been appreciated for millennia. Recent research has clarified that these insights and abilities represent a form of intelligence largely distinct from the logical, mathematical, and reasoning abilities measured by most intelligence and aptitude tests.

As you may have observed, someone can

perform exceptionally well on paper-and-pencil tests yet lack good judgment in personal relationships and social understanding. Conversely, another person may struggle with analytical reasoning tasks but have a strong sense of self and an exceptional ability to understand and get along with others. There are different ways of being intelligent—different types of intelligence.

Various researchers have described forms of intelligence that are largely separate from the reasoning abilities typically measured by IQ tests. Emotional Intelligence, or EQ, reflects the ability to perceive, understand, regulate, and use emotional information in ourselves and others. This type of intelligence enables people to better assess situations, empathize, and respond appropriately. EQ is closely related to what others have referred to as practical intelligence, street smarts, or simply social skills. In his bestselling book *Emotional Intelligence*, Daniel Goleman (1995) makes a strong case for why emotional intelligence can matter more in life than IQ.

People who understand themselves and who can accurately and deeply understand others are better equipped to make sound decisions and maintain healthy relationships. This has clear implications for managing both current and future stress. The American Psychological Association (2010) described several intervention trials with children. Those who were taught a combination of social awareness and emotional regulation skills showed significant improvements across academic and mental health measures compared to peers who did not receive such training. Not just the outcome, but the very fact that children were able to become more socially aware and gain better control of their emotions shows that this type of intelligence is open to modification and makes a strong, positive impact.

The primary pathway to self-discovery combines experience with personal observation. We learn about ourselves through our interactions with challenges and by noticing how we behave and are treated in relationships. We find out what we like and don't like and what we're naturally good at (or not) by trying a variety of things. We also observe how others are doing and make comparisons that influence our sense of how we're doing - and our place in the world.

Self-knowledge is information that can be put to practical use. Imagine someone routinely coming home from work absolutely starving (figuratively speaking) and immediately reaching for the potato chips or cookies on the counter - foods they find almost irresistible. If, instead, they had eaten an apple or an energy bar *before* arriving home, their blood sugar would be higher, and they wouldn't feel ravenous. Additionally, if they didn't keep chips or cookies in the house, they'd be more likely to reach for or prepare something healthier. A little planning, combined with self-knowledge, goes a long way.

Journaling Helps

Everyone experiences changes in their moods and in what occupies their thoughts. People also commonly have hopes and fears for the future, and many have gone through troubling experiences in their lives. However, not everyone takes time to reflect on or express what has happened or is happening in their life. Becoming more aware of our thoughts, feelings, and actions is a necessary first step toward gaining greater control over them in desired ways.

Journals provide a judgment-free space to express your thoughts. Writing in a journal is a good way to connect more deeply with your feelings and explore your options. It encourages personal exploration and can lead to increased awareness and improved coping. Both active engagement in life and paying attention to our experiences promote self-discovery. Keeping a journal can support this process by offering a space for reflection and for planning future responses. Indeed, writing out how we're specifically going to meet a challenge or accomplish a goal helps to foster action and positive expectations.

Research has shown that expectations matter. People who strongly expect to succeed at a specific goal (called self-efficacy expectations) tend to try harder and persist longer than those who aren't so sure they can succeed. As a consequence of greater effort and persistence, they succeed more often. Albert Bandura (1977) was instrumental in developing the social-cognitive theory that underlies today's cognitive-behavioral psychology and the power of expectations to influence effort, persistence, and success.

Our expectations for success at a specific task or goal are subject to change, though, and are most powerfully influenced by direct experience and our observations. Direct experiences have the strongest influence on personal expectations of success. Thus, expectations can improve as effectiveness improves, whether through training or practice, for example. Direct experience is not only the most powerful factor influencing self-efficacy expectations; it is also the factor we have the most control over. Breaking large projects and goals into smaller, concrete steps makes them easier to approach. Then, by succeeding at small, initial steps, we build our confidence for the next step and the next step.

Observing others also can influence our personal expectations for success. And that's particularly true if we perceive the person we're observing as being similar to ourselves. Seeing someone who is already highly skilled perform a difficult task may not influence our personal expectations for succeeding at that same task, but seeing someone we think is just like us makes a difference. It's along the line of "Oh, if they can do it, I should do fine too."

Our ability to be influenced by people we see as similar to ourselves also highlights the importance of exposure to positive role models. As children grow up, if they do not see people whom they view as being similar to themselves succeeding in school and in life, it can limit their imaginations. It is easier for people to create images of having a successful outcome if they know it can be done. When people see others whom they view as similar to themselves being successful, it becomes easier to imagine being successful, too. Our beliefs and inner dialogues both reflect and influence our expectations and emotions, and are open to modification: A subject that we will turn to next.

Chapter 3
A Positive Outlook

Stress reactions and emotions aren't under our direct, conscious control. We can't choose our feelings in the same way that we can choose to voice an opinion. However, our beliefs, expectations, and thoughts can still trigger or calm the responses of our emotional brain. What feels stressful to one person (and how stressful it feels) largely depends on how we think about and interpret events, meaning how we *perceive* the situation. One person stuck in traffic may see it as no big deal and spend the time lost in pleasant daydreams. As a result, they feel little, if any, stress from the traffic jam. Another person with no greater need to get anywhere quickly may interpret the same traffic as a major inconvenience and get very stressed.

Some people talk to themselves out loud at times, and nearly all young children do this while playing alone. However, all of us talk silently to ourselves in our minds. We carry on inner conversations throughout the day. Many of these thoughts are about small, everyday things, like, "Hmm, my shoelace feels loose. Maybe I should stop and re-tie it." Such conversations take place in our heads all the time and usually don't spark an emotional reaction or influence our life direction. But some of our inner conversations matter much more.

We are all creatures of habit. All of us develop and maintain a sense of how the world works, who we are, and what is in store for us. Our inner dialogues reflect and reinforce these belief systems, as well as become deeply ingrained habits. We tend to interpret events, think about ourselves, focus on certain parts of life, and predict outcomes in *habitual* ways. This is completely normal, but not always helpful. If the mental framework we use to understand the world and ourselves leans toward the negative, it can push us toward negative emotions and unhelpful behaviors. On the other hand, a more positive inner dialogue helps us build and maintain a positive self-image and leads to better feelings and more constructive behavior.

What is a Positive Outlook?

A positive outlook reflects the mental habit of commonly thinking in ways that lead to constructive actions and positive feelings, and infrequently thinking in ways that lead to ineffective actions and bad feelings. Positive and negative thinking both affect how we feel and function, but in different ways.

Emotionally, we're often in a neutral state. We don't automatically feel a sense of pride or joy just because nothing bad is happening at the moment. It's the presence of positive thoughts and experiences that lift us out of the neutral zone and bring about good feelings. Positive emotions, like love, pride, compassion, joy, and caring, stem from the presence of positive thinking and experiences, not just the absence of negativity. Unexpectedly finding a cool looking shell on a beach walk might make us happy, but not finding something we didn't expect to find anyway won't elicit negative feelings.

Conversely, negative emotions are elicited by negative thoughts and experiences and not simply by an absence of positive thoughts or events at that moment. For instance, getting honked at might elicit negative feelings, but not getting honked at doesn't elicit positive emotions. It's negative thoughts and experiences that take us out of our neutral emotional state in the opposite direction, eliciting negative feelings.

Of course, sometimes the switch from one emotional state to another can happen abruptly. We don't always get a chance to return to a neutral, unemotional state. Still, the independence of positive and negative feeling states holds true, and each is elicited separately by different events and thoughts.

So, it's not just experiences that affect emotions, but how we perceive experiences, and how we think about ourselves and form expectations that also greatly impact our emotions. Thinking styles are powerful influences in our lives, in large part because they are habitual and pervasive. No matter where we go or what we are trying to accomplish, our habitual ways of thinking are present, coloring our emotions, decisions, and outcomes.

Why does one student with a question raise their hand in class while another stays silent? Often, the student who stays quiet is having an internal conversation, talking themselves out of speaking up. They might be questioning whether their question is good enough or worrying about what others will think. Likewise, people who take action to solve problems tend to have a very different kind of self-talk compared to those who feel stuck, stressed, or helpless.

In every area of life, our thinking styles affect what we do, say, and feel. Research suggests that happy, well-adjusted people have positive thoughts that occur about twice as commonly as negative thoughts. In contrast, that same line of research found that people who struggle with depression or anxiety tend to have as many or more negative thoughts than positive ones. Everyone experiences both types of thoughts, but a preponderance of negative thoughts equates to having more negative emotions and less constructive actions.

Another reason that thinking styles are so important is that they provide a place to effect change. It is pretty much useless to tell someone to stop feeling anxious, angry, or sad. People are not in direct control of their emotions and can't just turn them on or off like a light switch. However, because thoughts and feelings go hand in hand, redirecting thinking provides a powerful tool for influencing emotions along with all their motivational capacity. This idea is at the heart of a type of therapy called *cognitive psychotherapy*, which helps people improve their emotional well-being by changing their thinking patterns.

Characteristics of Positive Thinking

Positive thinking habits have four key features: optimism, control-orientation, open-mindedness, and self-enhancement. While we'll discuss each separately, it's important to remember they often overlap and work together.

- Optimism:

This is a core element of a positive outlook. An optimist is someone who:

1. Focuses more on the good in life.
2. Holds positive expectations for the future.

Seeing the good in life is a characteristic of optimists that is best captured by the classic notion that an optimist sees the glass as half full, while a pessimist sees it as half empty. While optimists aren't usually oblivious to the negative aspects of the world, such as pollution, crime, greed, loneliness, racism, terrorists, world hunger, etc., they choose not to dwell on them unproductively. Instead, they direct their attention toward the good that the same world holds, such as beauty, love, fun, opportunities, kindness, etc. While the world holds both good and bad, optimists see more of the good.

Positive expectations are another defining feature of an optimist. Optimists expect to succeed and believe that most things will turn out well. By maintaining positive yet realistic expectations for their future, they are able to make stronger commitments to their goals and sustain greater effort. This, in turn, leads to better physical and emotional health, as well as higher rates of success.

This type of optimism is not mere wishful thinking. It's important to distinguish between optimism, as defined here, and what is known as *naive* or *unrealistic optimism*. When people expect good things to happen despite clear evidence to the contrary, it is considered naive (or unrealistic) optimism.

While optimism has been linked in numerous studies to a wide variety of desirable outcomes, such as goal attainment, naive optimism is generally unrelated to success across life's various domains. For example, a person who engages in unprotected sex because they believe they won't be "unlucky" enough to get a sexually transmitted disease is being naively optimistic. Naive optimism

76

undermines motivation and constructive action. In contrast, true optimists expect good outcomes *because* they recognize and take control of the factors that influence those outcomes.

• **Control-Oriented:**

Another defining feature of positive thinking is that it is control-oriented, with thoughts focused on aspects where they will do some good. By concentrating on areas where they can exert control, positive thinkers are more likely to resolve problems and setbacks as well as feel better throughout the process. Thinking in terms of *"What can I do that will help?"* promotes a proactive mindset. Rather than simply reacting to events, positive thinkers anticipate future needs and problems and take action in advance. This forward-thinking approach provides them with a greater sense of control and effectiveness than merely responding to immediate demands.

• Open-mindedness

Open-mindedness is the third defining feature of positive thinking. It involves interpreting events, options, and people in flexible ways. Life is rarely black and white, and those who view it in rigid terms are often at a disadvantage. Open-mindedness allows people to be more trusting and accepting rather than suspicious and rejecting. This mental flexibility also supports better problem-solving by helping people recognize different paths forward and understand when to take action versus when to let something go.

• Self-enhancement

Self-enhancement is the final defining feature of positive thinking. It reflects the tendency to interpret self-relevant events in ways that preserve motivation, self-esteem, and positive emotions - even in the face of occasional setbacks or failures. For example, if a student gets a low test score and decides it was because they didn't study enough, they're more likely to be motivated to prepare better next time. But if they blame it on a lack of ability, they may just give up. Interpreting events to ourselves in ways that lead to better feelings and more constructive actions is known as an optimistic explanatory style.

Negative thinking habits also have four defining features, which are largely the opposite of those found in positive thinking. These include pessimism, passive orientation, closed-mindedness, and self-denigration. These characteristics are contrasted in the table below.

Positive Thinking Characteristics

Optimism: Expecting good outcomes and focusing on the positive aspects of life.

Control-Oriented: Focusing thoughts on areas where control can be exercised to advance life plans and solve problems.

Open-Mindedness: Thinking flexibly promotes effective problem solving and being more accepting of differences in opinions and choices.

Self-Enhancing: Interpreting situations and setbacks in ways that support healthy self-esteem and lead to constructive responses and feelings. Recognizes and values personal strengths and successes.

Negative Thinking Characteristics

Pessimism: Expecting negative outcomes and focusing on the negative aspects of life.

Passive Orientation: Focusing on feelings of powerlessness or victimhood, often leading to coping strategies like escape, denial, or passive suffering.

Closed-Mindedness: Rigid, categorical thinking limits problem solving and fosters over-generalization.

Self-Denigrating: Interpreting situations and setbacks in ways that reinforce low self-esteem and lead to negative feelings and behaviors. Engages in self-criticism while overlooking personal strengths.

Thoughts and Feelings Go Together in Specific Ways

Specific kinds of thinking are linked to specific emotional reactions. For example, when someone feels anxious, they're usually having worrisome thoughts. When someone is angry, they're likely thinking angry thoughts.

Of course, there are situations where feelings of anxiety or anger are legitimate and understandable responses to a specific situation. However, a person with negative thinking habits experiences negative emotions too frequently and too easily.

A person who is often angry or easily irritated is likely interpreting and thinking about things in ways that trigger that particular emotional state. This is clearly different from the mindset of a positive thinker, but it also differs from that of other types of negative thinkers. For example, a negative thinker who tends to worry may often feel anxious but rarely have angry thoughts and, therefore, rarely feel angry. Conversely, someone who is often and easily irritated may seldom engage in anxiety-inducing thoughts and, as a result, rarely feel anxious.

Specific thoughts lead to specific emotions. Because occasional negative feelings and events are a normal part of life, even someone with a very positive outlook will sometimes have negative thoughts. However, positive thinkers are less likely to think negatively about trivial matters or to dwell on negative thoughts in unproductive ways.

How Thinking Habits Get Started

The tendency to react strongly to stress and to experience negative emotions such as anger and anxiety has a genetic component. Some people are born more prone to negative emotions than others, and these emotions have their cognitive counterparts. Thoughts and feelings go together. However, just as people can overcome inborn shyness or aggressive tendencies with conscious effort, a genetically based predisposition toward negative thinking can also be lessened through deliberate effort.

In addition to genetic influences, thinking habits also reflect experience, and some types of learning experiences are more powerful than others. People are exposed to role models, may be purposely taught certain beliefs, and are often reinforced for expressing "the right" viewpoints or attitudes. These belief systems then become reflected in how people think about events and choices.

Thinking habits based on deeply ingrained beliefs or emotionally charged learning experiences can be harder to change. For example, a young child who is neglected and living in an unstable environment may come to erroneously believe that they are powerless, inferior, or unworthy of love. Just like a strong genetic tendency, deep emotional learning from early life can be tough to work through as an adult, but clearly doable and important enough to be worth the time and effort.

How to Develop a Positive Outlook

Thinking styles influence our experiences, but our experiences also shape the types of thoughts we are likely to have. It is much easier to think positively when we are creating and experiencing positive life circumstances. Consequently, part of developing a more positive outlook involves exercising greater control over our lives. It's easier to build positive thinking habits when we are also taking steps to move our lives forward in our desired ways.

Let's use a student with pronounced test-taking anxiety to illustrate this principle. Since anxiety is related to worrisome thinking, we can imagine this student filling their mind with all sorts of negative predictions and "what if?" scenarios that trigger anxiety. From a purely cognitive intervention model, the student might be taught to counter those thoughts with more positive ones, such as:

"I'm well-prepared and just need to relax."

"This nervous energy means I care and will do fine."

But on the other hand, what if this student hasn't prepared for the test at all? Would saying *"I'll do fine, I'm well-prepared"* significantly reduce their anxiety? Not likely. Cognitive strategies like these work best when the calming thoughts ring true. A test-anxious student who begins preparing well in advance before the anxiety builds up is in a much better position to use positive thinking strategies effectively to manage their anxiety. Positive thinking works best when it is reality-based and rings true.

Five Steps to a More Positive Outlook

Shifting to a more positive inner dialogue can be broken down into five steps, outlined below. Each step is examined in more detail afterward:

1. Become aware of inner dialogues and see them as choices.
2. Assess whether your thinking is negatively biased.
3. Challenge negatively skewed thoughts and predictions.
4. Replace negative thoughts with more rational and adaptive ones.
5. Continue practicing to make positive thinking habitual.

Step One: Become Aware of Inner Dialogues and See Them as Choices

A common reason people get stuck in negative thought patterns is that they're unaware that there are other ways of interpreting their situation. If you ask someone stuck in traffic or waiting for a late bus why they're so angry, they'd probably be surprised by your question. They might respond, perhaps angrily, "I'm mad because the bus is late," or "Because the traffic isn't moving."

It's extremely unlikely they would say, "I'm upset because I'm blowing this out of proportion and working myself up over something small." No, if they had that much insight, they'd be using it. We generally accept our perceptions and interpretations of events as reality and react accordingly. Learning to notice how we talk ourselves into certain moods or reactions is the first step in shifting toward a more positive perspective.

Awareness of your self-talk does **not** require constant analysis. You could drive yourself crazy trying to examine every inner conversation. Fortunately, you don't have to. Instead, pay particular attention to your inner dialogue during key moments, such as when you're making an important decision or experiencing a negative emotional state. That's when it's most helpful to pause and ask, "What am I telling myself right now?"

Step Two: Assess Whether Your Thinking is Negatively Biased

Ask yourself whether your current way of thinking is:

1. Helping you take constructive action, or
2. Helping you feel better.

Unless you can honestly answer "yes" to at least one of these questions, there's an opportunity to improve your inner dialogue.

When possible, write out your negative thoughts exactly as you're thinking them. Writing out your thoughts has several benefits. Sometimes, simply seeing our thoughts on paper can help us recognize that we're being overly negative. In addition, writing them down allows you to return to them later. In the heat of the moment, it can be difficult to think positively, even when you try. By recording your negative thoughts, you give yourself the chance to revisit them later when you're in a better frame of mind and more capable of seeing the situation and your options more constructively.

Step Three: Challenge Negatively Skewed Thoughts and Predictions

Some negative thinking may be obvious, such as when someone is clearly making a mountain out of a molehill. Many minor hassles can be made less stressful by reminding ourselves, *"This is temporary,"* or *"This isn't a big deal."* However, because thinking reflects underlying beliefs and expectations, it is not always so clear-cut. Step Three may involve challenging firmly held beliefs, not just obvious negativity.

For instance, someone who believes they failed a test because they're "not smart enough" may not view this as negative thinking; they may see it as the sad truth. Consequently, they might also believe that studying more for the next test won't help because they've identified their problem as low intelligence rather than insufficient effort. Negative thinking can stem from such deeply rooted beliefs that a person may defend these thoughts, even when others try to convince them otherwise.

Step Three, then, may involve challenging beliefs and self-judgments that feel true. Just because something feels familiar doesn't mean it's right. Remember: if your thinking isn't helping you feel better or leading to constructive action, then there's room for improvement - so challenge it!

Step Four: Replace Negative Thinking with More Rational and Adaptive Thoughts

In situations where direct action can help, focusing your thoughts on what you *can do* moves you out of a passive, negative mindset. This approach works for several reasons. First, when you focus on what you can do, you're not focusing on your negative thoughts. Trying to rid your mind of negativity by clearing it completely is nearly impossible, especially when you're upset. When upset, focusing your thoughts on what you can do gives you something concrete to think about, which helps displace negativity.

Second, focusing on what we can do helps improve our expectations by reminding us that we have control and can get through the situation.

Step four also includes actively replacing negatively skewed thoughts with thoughts that lead to better feelings. For example, research shows that minor hassles are a significant source of stress, affecting both our emotional and physical well-being. Coping with minor hassles is less about taking action and more about being accepting and thinking about them in a rational way, along the lines of reminding ourselves that this will pass and it's no big deal. We all overreact from time to time. Catching that overreaction and shifting to a more reasonable thought process helps reduce stress and improve emotional outcomes.

There are many potential situations where shifting to a more accepting or optimistic inner dialogue can lead to better feelings as well as better behavior. If you've written down negative thoughts in Step Two, now is the time to counter them on paper. You don't want to come up with great insights on how to think more positively, only to forget them the next time the same situation comes up. By writing down both negative and alternative positive thoughts, you'll have something to refer back to when needed. Writing aids memory and retention. Just as it helps with studying, it also helps with developing positive thinking habits.

Step Five: Continue Practicing to Make Positive Thinking Habitual

Deeply ingrained habits take time to change, and it's normal to slip back into old, familiar thought patterns from time to time. Changing habits isn't a race. Just remember that your patience and persistence will pay off over time. Positive thinking works best when it's combined with positive action and effective communication.

Chapter 4
Effective Communication

Research suggests that no other aspect of life has a more powerful influence on our emotional well-being than relationships. And because social interaction and social standing are so important to us, they are also ripe for stress when they are less than satisfactory. It's not just open conflict that is stressful, though. We can react with stress to a wide variety of social interactions, especially when we feel we're not being treated fairly or when our desire to be liked, respected, or loved is unmet. It is also stressful when we don't know what to say or how to say it, or if we're unsure whether we should say anything at all. And while no one wants to look foolish, fear of embarrassment is a frequent source of stress for people who are socially anxious. Interpersonal stress is common, and communication skills play a key role in managing its many forms.

Whether it's getting our questions answered, asking for help, or resolving—or even avoiding—conflicts, many situations can trigger heightened stress if our communication skills aren't strong enough to handle them. Even other active coping strategies, such as planning for our future and managing our time, often include the need for direct communication, like saying "no" to invitations when we need to finish an important project first. Communication skills play a central role in actively coping with stress. However, the benefits and functions of effective communication go beyond stress management.

Communication not only helps us meet our social needs and share our feelings, but it also helps us understand others better and respond in the right way. When we develop good communication skills, we not only improve our chances of being treated fairly and with respect but also of developing deeper and more satisfying relationships, whether casual or intimate. And because our social interactions and the quality of our relationships are so central to our sense of self and well-being, the development of effective communication skills is one of the most concrete ways a person can improve their self-esteem and sense of control. Good communication skills enhance our resiliency and self-esteem. Effective communication is also a skill that anyone can markedly improve with practice and effort.

If you were born with an extroverted (socially outgoing) personality and grew up in an environment where effective communication patterns were role-modeled and reinforced, then effective communication skills have likely come easily to you. Yet even people with generally strong communication skills can find communicating effectively difficult at times and in certain circumstances. Can even bright, articulate people get into the same unproductive arguments again and again? You bet. Although we communicate all the time, communicating is more complex than it may appear to be on the surface.

The Complexity of Communication

Let's begin with a simple example. Jessica says to Michael, "I can't get together this weekend. I've got to study." At first glance, this sounds like a straightforward, brief communication. But is it really that simple?

If Jessica and Michael have a healthy relationship, whether romantic or platonic, and if occasionally prioritizing schoolwork is normal for them, then yes, this message may be interpreted as routine and unproblematic. However, context is important.

Would this message still seem straightforward if you knew they'd recently been having relationship troubles? What if Michael had an old friend visiting from out of town, whom Jessica doesn't like? What if her tone was cold or distant? What if they had already made weekend plans, and she was canceling at the last possible moment? Or what if Michael is particularly insecure or jealous?

Many factors influence how a message is interpreted. Background factors like those mentioned above are just a few of many 'what if?' situations that can influence how a message is understood or delivered. In this example, Michael might interpret Jessica's message in a number of different ways, depending on the dynamics between them.

At its most basic, communication involves two people who alternate roles as sender and receiver. Effective communication means being both a clear sender and a receptive, perceptive receiver. But it's more complex than just using and understanding words. Consider a simple statement like, "That outfit looks great on you." Depending on the context, it might genuinely mean what it says, or it could be a manipulative sales tactic, like "I'll say anything to make a sale." Many different factors and reasons affect what and how people communicate. Because of this, we pay attention to many signals to try to understand messages correctly.

Now, let's look at some common factors that

affect both the sender and receiver during communication, starting with non-verbal cues.

Non-verbal Cues

Communication is not limited to the verbal content, i.e., the specific words spoken, but also includes *how* something is said. For example, if someone you're getting to know makes a comment that might be a joke, you'll likely rely on non-verbal signals, such as facial expressions or tone, to interpret the meaning.

Non-verbal communication includes all the cues that help convey a message besides the actual words. Words spoken in a cold, harsh, or sarcastic tone will be understood very differently than the same words delivered in a warm or joking tone. Posture, eye contact, facial expressions, and other body language aspects are important non-verbal cues that transmit meaningful information. Non-verbal cues help us better understand communication and are influential enough to override the verbal message. If a friend tells you, "I'm not upset," but their tone, volume, and body language suggest otherwise, which are you more likely to believe—their words or all their non-verbal cues?

Non-verbal communication can also take place in the absence of a verbal message. People often "pick up on" what someone is feeling or wanting without anything being explicitly said. A smile from across the room can convey a great deal of information without a single word. The ability to interpret these subtle signals and 'read people,' like what someone wants or feels, is part of what's known as *emotional intelligence*.

However, it's important not to confuse this with mind-reading. Just because non-verbal communication is powerful doesn't mean we should expect people to automatically know what we're thinking or feeling. Rather, it highlights how much information is often communicated without words. When non-verbal cues are missing, as is common in email or text, it becomes much harder to accurately gauge someone's mood or intent.

Context

Context heavily influences how we interpret messages. A joke may seem funnier at a lively party than in a quiet office. You might interpret a reminder or suggestion by a coworker differently if it's offered just as your boss passes by. And a discussion of something personal with a close friend might be completely comfortable in a private setting, but quite uncomfortable in a crowded elevator.

Even written communication relies on context. For example, when handwritten quickly, the letter "s" and the number "5" can look quite similar. We usually rely on surrounding information to make the correct interpretation, like a sequence of numbers likely contains a "5" while a sequence of letters points to an "s."

Context can be so powerful that it might override the message itself. In environments with loud background noise or numerous distractions, the intended message can easily be lost or misinterpreted.

Mood

Have you ever said something completely innocent, only to have it taken the wrong way because the other person was in a bad mood? Or did you notice your own words come out sharper than intended because you were in a bad mood?

We're all human, and we all do this type of thing at times. The mood of the sender or the receiver can influence how a message is sent and how it is interpreted. When both sender and receiver are in a bad mood, communication can get off track even more quickly.

Cultural Norms

Culture affects communication beyond the actual words and language used. In individualistic cultures like the United States, interrupting a speaker to ask a question may be seen as a sign of engagement. However, in many collectivist cultures where harmony is prioritized, such interruptions would more likely be considered rude. Likewise, how readily emotions are expressed, how close people stand, their volume, and whether people touch or use hand gestures are all factors affecting communication that can vary culturally. Consequently, people of different cultures may send and receive messages differently. As we explore communication styles further, we'll look at how cultural differences can be acknowledged and accommodated.

Beliefs

Would you interact differently with someone you believe could help you achieve your career goals? Beliefs influence not only how we approach a conversation but also how we interpret messages. A compliment from someone we trust and admire feels different than the same compliment from someone we suspect has ulterior motives.

Expectations

Expectations are another form of belief. For instance, if someone expects others to judge them harshly, they may stay silent instead of asking a question or sharing an idea. Similarly, you might not share personal information with someone who you expect to be judgmental and put you down. Beliefs and expectations color both how messages are sent and how they're received.

Unshared Meaning

People have unique background experiences that can influence how they communicate and how they interpret certain messages. Because of these experiential differences, a loud and intense conversation might seem enthusiastic to one person but feel like the start of a fight to another. Likewise, specific words that are neutral or positive to most people might be perceived negatively by someone because of their particular history. Being called a "jock" might be a compliment to someone proud of their athletic identity, but to someone who grew up hearing that term used to imply low intelligence or poor social skills, it could feel like a slight.

When people don't share the same understanding of words or non-verbal cues, communication can break down.

Attention

For a message to be understood, the receiver must be paying attention. As obvious as this may seem, it is nonetheless fairly common for a person's attention to drift off. Have you ever stopped listening to someone as they were talking and instead started planning in your head what you were going to say? Sounds may get in our ears, but for a message to be understood, it has to be attended to and actively processed.

The Receiving Side of Effective Communication

If you are talking about something very personal and the other person shows no interest, would you continue? Like most people, you would be more likely to continue speaking if the person listening was encouraging and showed interest. You might also find it much more satisfying. Active listening is a key ingredient of effective communication. It entails paying attention to the other person's non-verbal cues as well as the spoken words and giving off cues in return that reveal interest in fully understanding their message. The active listening process not only aids understanding on the part of the receiver but also helps the sender feel validated and understood, which helps keep communication on track and productive. Two-way communication is shaped by both the verbal and non-verbal cues of the receiver, just as much as the sender.

When we're trying to communicate something we consider important, we naturally look for cues to see how our message is being received. Someone who is actively listening will give off signals that indicate they're taking our message seriously. These cues include appearing attentive, nodding or showing other signs of understanding, and asking thoughtful questions that reflect interest in what we're saying. Even if the receiver isn't saying much verbally, they are often communicating a great deal non-verbally. By signaling that they are paying attention and trying

112

to understand, they convey interest and respect, both of which help keep a conversation on track.

In contrast, imagine you're trying to share something important with someone who doesn't seem to be listening. Perhaps they don't look at you and appear distracted, or wear a bored or dismissive expression on their face. Maybe they don't ask any questions about your thoughts or feelings, and instead cut you off to share what they think. Being ignored, talked over, or dismissed doesn't feel good and can damage relationships.

In conversations like these, it is not just the sender but the receiver as well who is communicating a great deal, mostly non-verbally. The point is that we are all both senders and receivers. Effective communication isn't just about expressing ourselves clearly; it also requires being an active listener.

Reflective Listening

Reflective listening is a type of active listening in which the listener reflects back on what they understand the speaker to be saying or feeling. For example, if someone describes a rough day at work followed by a frustrating commute, a reflective response might be, *"Wow, sounds like you really had one of those days."* Reflective statements help show someone that they are being actively listened to.

In addition, reflective statements can help both parties clarify messages. When the listener reflects on their understanding, the speaker has an opportunity to confirm their accuracy or provide clarification if the interpretation is off. That helps both parties.

Active Listening Does Not Require Agreement

Even when someone already knows they are going to say "no" or otherwise disagree, active listening still helps. Active listening provides powerful cues to let the sender know they are being taken seriously. People who are listened to actively in this manner are more likely to feel respected, understood, cared about, and validated. This sets the stage for more positive feelings between the involved parties, even if they ultimately continue to disagree about the issue at hand. It's important to remember that active listening does not require the listener to agree or offer help. Agreeing or offering help is separate from the act of active listening.

There are many casual interactions where the

sender doesn't really require much feedback or cues that serve to demonstrate clear interest and concern. In casual conversations and interchanges between people who know and like each other well, formal rules of effective communication are often broken without causing a problem. For example, a good friend might interpret and react to a shrug of the shoulders as a perfectly adequate response to a message in some circumstances.

In long-term relationships with spouses, family, and old friends, interactions often become far less formal than they are within less established relationships. However, in situations that are more ambiguous, complex, or emotionally difficult, active and reflective listening can help. What is important is the ability to detect when a conversation requires a higher level of listening and then go into active listening mode at those times. For some, this awareness and response come naturally. For others, it takes conscious effort and practice.

Chapter 5
Communication Styles

How we communicate with others as the sender involves both verbal and non-verbal elements and can be loosely categorized into three styles: passive, assertive, and aggressive communication.

- Passive communication involves failing to express what we truly want, think, or feel.

- Assertive communication means expressing our thoughts, desires, and feelings clearly while respecting others' needs and emotions.

- Aggressive communication is expressing what we want, think, or feel without regard for the rights or feelings of others.

These styles can be seen as points along a continuum, with passive communication on one end, aggressive communication on the other, and assertive communication in the balanced center.

Understanding the differences between these styles is the first step toward becoming a more effective communicator. It is the assertive middle ground that we should aim for in the vast majority of communication situations. Passive communication and aggressive communication are much less effective and satisfying in terms of the outcomes they tend to yield.

Styles of Communication: Passive, assertive, and aggressive communications form a continuum. Each type of communication includes both verbal and non-verbal elements.

PASSIVE COMMUNICATION

Verbal: Failing to verbalize directly in words what we want, think, and feel.

For example, saying "yes" when we want to say "no" or not speaking up when we have a question.

Non-verbal: Using a tone, volume, and body language that is inconsistent with or undermines what we really think and feel

For example, a hesitant voice and downcast eyes.

ASSERTIVE COMMUNICATION

Verbal: Expressing our thoughts, desires, and feelings directly while showing consideration for others'rights and feelings.

For example, saying "no"firmly yet sensitively.

Non-verbal: Using tone, volume, and body language consistent with the message that we want to convey.

For example, a steady voiceand good eye contact.

AGGRESSIVE COMMUNICATION

Verbal: Communicating what we want, think, and feel without consideration for the rights and feelings of others.

For example, using verbal threats and put-downs.

Non-verbal: Using tone, volume, and body language that is threatening or demeaning to the other person.

For example, yelling, glaring, and finger-pointing.n.

121

Passive Communication

In certain situations, even people with generally good communication skills may find it difficult and uncomfortable to say what they want, think, or feel in a direct manner. For others, passive communication is a more pervasive pattern that interferes with effective social functioning. Passive communication can reveal itself in many ways, both verbally and non-verbally. For example, speaking in a weak or hesitant voice conveys a lack of confidence, regardless of the words being spoken. Similarly, downcast or averted eye contact may suggest passivity and low confidence, although, in some cultures, this may instead be a sign of respect.

For a message to be taken seriously, the verbal and non-verbal components should align. Passive communication often fails to convey a "serious" message because the cues are inconsistent or unclear.

Rather than getting right to the point, someone communicating in a passive mode may ramble, hint, or make excuses. For instance, rather than saying, *"I really don't want to go to the mall (or lake, or museum),"* they might say, *"What if it's crowded?"* or *"Gee, it's so hot today."* These indirect comments are far less effective than a clear, honest statement. By avoiding direct expression, the passive communicator often experiences increased stress and uncertainty. Friends can also become frustrated with someone who doesn't say what they really think or feel.

Making excuses is another common form of passive, indirect communication. While polite excuses are common and sometimes completely appropriate, habitual excuse-making can lead to complications. For example, someone might say, *"Oh, I can't this weekend, my mom's visiting,"* instead of simply and politely declining an unwanted invitation. If the other person responds with, *"No problem, I'll change the tickets to next weekend,"* or *"Can I stop by? I'd love to meet your mom,"* the situation becomes awkward. Indirect communication like this is dishonest and, when discovered, can damage relationships.

Saying nothing can also reflect a passive communication style when it is done out of fear. Of course, there are valid reasons to remain silent, such as preferring reflection or simply having nothing to add. However, not speaking up by choice is different from not speaking up out of fear. Because of concerns that what they say might

124

be viewed or reacted to in a negative manner by others, passive communicators sometimes opt to say nothing at all.

For example, a fearful student might avoid asking a question in class, despite really wanting clarification. Remaining silent in this way doesn't help people meet their needs and may be misinterpreted as a lack of interest or competence in both personal and professional contexts. In addition, people who fail to stand up for their rights are more likely to be taken advantage of by others and to be treated less respectfully.

Another form of passive communication involves putting oneself down or apologizing unnecessarily. This style is often linked to low self-esteem and self-denigrating thought patterns. People who see themselves as inferior may find it difficult to speak up or communicate on equal footing. Unfortunately, passive, self-critical communication tends to provoke more negative responses from others, reinforcing feelings of inadequacy and social rejection. Therefore, improving both our thinking and our communication patterns are complementary steps toward building greater confidence and self-esteem.

Consequences of Passive Communication

Depending on the number and type of situations where passive communication is problematic, it can lead to any or all of the following consequences:

Decreased Ability to Get Needs and Wishes Met:

Because we are highly social beings, taking charge of our lives often requires assertive communication. Passive communication can lead to missed opportunities for desired outcomes and a greater frequency of undesired ones. Speaking up for ourselves is an essential part of self-determination.

Increased Likelihood of Negative Emotions:

When communication fails to effectively meet personal needs, passive communicators are more likely to experience increased stress, anxiety, uncertainty, and frustration. Imagine how frequently someone might feel stressed if they are unable to say "no" to unwanted invitations or to a supervisor's work request when already overcommitted.

Poor Impressions:

Passive communication may elicit less positive reactions from others, especially strangers, who might interpret silence or passivity as a lack of knowledge or interest. Since we all make assumptions based on what we see and hear, and others do the same with us, someone who doesn't speak up assertively may be misunderstood or judged negatively in some circumstances.

Decreased Likelihood of Achieving Healthy Self-Esteem:

Self-esteem is built, in part, by seeing ourselves function effectively and by being treated well by others. Passive communication can interfere with both of these experiences. Negative reactions to passivity may reinforce beliefs that one's thoughts and feelings aren't as important as those of others, further damaging self-esteem.

Reduced Chances of Building or Deepening Relationships:

Relationships are unlikely to deepen without the sharing of genuine thoughts and emotions. A person who focuses solely on pleasing others while withholding personal opinions, desires, or feelings limits the kind of relationships they can form. Others don't get a chance to truly know them. Importantly, passivity is not the same as being nice. In fact, it can create barriers to connection. As we will see later in this chapter, a person can be both nice and polite while still expressing their opinions and emotions with directness and honesty.

Passive Communication Can **Lead to Aggressive Communication**

When passive communicators consistently fail to speak up, frustration often builds over time. Unfortunately, bottling up feelings can result in an explosion when they are eventually expressed.

Imagine someone annoyed by a roommate's

habit of playing loud music in their adjoining bedroom. If they speak up early, perhaps the first time it happens, they might express their concern calmly and without anger. In this case, it's likely to come across as a simple request, nothing more.

But now, imagine that they avoid saying anything because they fear confrontation. The irritation builds over time and then may become strong enough to override their desire to avoid conflict. By that point, when they do speak up, the bottled-up frustration may come out as harsh or even aggressive communication. In this way, passive communication can ultimately lead to aggressive communication when repressed emotions boil over and override self-restraint.

Aggressive Communication

Aggressive communication means speaking in

a way that pushes your own opinions or feelings while ignoring or hurting other people's rights and feelings. Verbally, this style often includes harsh, threatening, or demeaning language. Statements like "Who asked you?" communicate disrespect and hostility.

Aggressive communication puts others on the defensive and frequently provokes negative emotions. While hurting others' feelings or provoking may sometimes be the goal of an aggressive communicator, it is often not intentional. Anyone can slip into using harsh or demeaning language, especially when upset or lacking effective communication skills. Let's look at the following example:

Lisa is upset with her roommate for leaving dirty dishes in the living room. Although Lisa's complaint is perfectly legitimate, her aggressive communication style creates unnecessary conflict. Instead of calmly addressing the issue by saying something like, "I find it frustrating when dishes are left in the living room. Can we make sure to clean up after ourselves?" Lisa lashes out. She calls her roommate a "slob" and accuses her of "expecting me to pick up after you all the time like I'm your mother."

Attacks on someone's character usually elicit a defensive response. It is easy for someone to reply to such an accusation with, "Oh yeah? Well, you do x, y, and z!" Aggressive communication often begets aggressive responses and is harmful to relationships.

While aggressive communication can be very direct and may work in some situations to achieve immediate goals, it comes with significant downsides. People who habitually communicate aggressively can quickly damage or lose friendships, romantic relationships, and professional ties.

Roots of Aggressive Communication

There are situations where an aggressive response may be justified. For example, firmly and loudly telling someone, *"Do not put your hands on me,"* can be a necessary and justified reaction in certain circumstances. But that is very different from someone who frequently reacts with aggression in everyday situations. Some people respond aggressively too quickly and too often. This tendency is often linked to impulsiveness.

Impulsiveness is acting without fully considering the consequences. It can amplify the likelihood of aggressive communication. Both aggressiveness and impulsivity have a partial genetic basis, but learned behavior plays a major role as well. Like someone born with a predisposition to shyness, a person inclined toward aggression or impulsivity can learn to manage these traits, but it often takes deliberate effort and practice.

Those with a quick temper or an impulsive nature must learn to slow down and think before reacting. For some, this might mean taking deep breaths and counting to ten (or more) before responding. This intentional pause creates space to consider not just *what* we want to say but *how* we want to say it.

Assertive Communication

Assertive communication involves clearly

expressing your thoughts, desires, and feelings while also respecting the rights and emotions of others. It includes both verbal and non-verbal elements that are consistent with one another. Non-verbal aspects of assertive communication include a relaxed body posture, a steady tone of voice, and making eye contact without staring or glaring.

Because assertive communication avoids mixed messages between words and body language, it tends to be easier to understand and often leads to more positive responses. However, this does not mean that assertive communication is an ironclad guarantee of a positive response. For example, someone who is angry or aggressive might still respond negatively, no matter how respectfully the message they heard was delivered. Assertive communication simply gives the best chance that your message will be taken seriously and responded to in a constructive way.

Distinguishing Passive, Assertive, and Aggressive Communication

The lines between passive, assertive, and aggressive communication aren't always clear. What one person sees as assertive, another might view as pushy or even aggressive. Similarly, what some might label as passive, others may see as polite or respectful.

The basic defining features of passive, assertive, and aggressive communication are readily distinguished from one another, but the exact boundaries are not. While this may add some confusion, it also offers the potential to find a particular communication style that best matches your values. This section aims to help clarify some of the flexibility within assertive communication and make it feel more approachable and natural.

Choosing When To Be Assertive

People can choose *when* to be assertive. In fact, we must. Someone who always has to put in their two cents and let everyone know what they think and want would come across as obnoxious. There are many situations where someone might choose *not* to verbalize exactly or directly what they think or feel for any number of valid reasons. What makes this different from passive communication is that it is a conscious choice.

There is a clear difference between choosing not to tell a host (when asked) that a dish they prepared was horrible and failing to voice a question out of fear. Being assertive gives people choices—and, with that, greater control. They can choose to speak up assertively in many situations and do so with comfort. An assertive person can also choose not to speak up when doing so would needlessly hurt or inconvenience another, or when they realize it's someone else's turn to speak or make a decision.

For example, telling a visiting relative or friend that you'd be happy to take them somewhere they're excited to go, even though you have no real desire to go there again, is not being passive if you're making a conscious choice to be giving. In that case, you're not being passive but simply prioritizing your relationship.

People can also choose *how* to be assertive. Assertive communication need not be so direct that it comes across as abrupt or insensitive. There's nothing passive about prefacing what we say in a way that helps the other person feel cared for and respected.

Take the situation of a good friend calling with an enthusiastic invitation to a museum visit on an upcoming weekend. If you can't go because you already have plans, you could just say, "Nope, I have other plans." While that is a clear response, it lacks warmth and empathy.

In a case like this, you can express appreciation for your friend's invitation and enthusiasm while still saying "no." For example, you can say, *"Oh, I can't. I'm already committed to doing something else. I'm sorry. We'll have to do something fun another weekend."* This response still conveys a firm *"no"* but will likely be perceived as kinder by your friend. You can be very firm and assertive yet still be warm and polite. Being assertive and being nice and sensitive are completely compatible.

Apologies can be another point of confusion when distinguishing between passive and assertive communication. Some apologies are unnecessary and signal a passive communication style. One doesn't have to apologize for having their own opinion. However, there are many times when apologizing is appropriate and completely aligned with being assertive. We all make mistakes, and a sincere apology can go a long way toward easing tension and setting the stage for positive dialogue. Apologies can also be offered while still holding firmly to one's position.

Imagine two friends getting into a nasty argument and canceling their plans because one of them arrived much later than planned. If they meet the next day to talk it over, it wouldn't be passive or an admission of guilt for either of them to begin with something like, *"I'm sorry the situation got out of hand yesterday,"* or *"I'm sorry for my part in this."*

Unnecessary apologizing is part of passive communication, but a sincere apology is not. Again, there is a great deal of cultural and stylistic freedom in how someone chooses to communicate assertively.

Cultural Values and Communication

Cultural values also influence how we communicate. Culture shapes communication by reinforcing certain patterns and defining what is considered proper or respectful.

Collectivist cultures, for example, prioritize relationship harmony over personal needs and are more likely to avoid direct confrontation, especially with elders or authority figures. College, in our society, is an example of a situation where students are encouraged to speak up for themselves and ask questions, even in the presence of an authority figure (the professor) and many strangers (the other students).

College is, therefore, a prime example of a social environment where conflict may arise between collectivist values and the communication expectations of an individualist society like our own.

Evidence suggests that people from collectivist cultures often feel less nervous or uncomfortable speaking up as they gain more time and experience. Fortunately, while acculturation may be part of the answer to resolving culturally based communication difficulties, it is not the only answer.

Prefacing as a Cultural Tool

Prefacing can serve as a bridge that allows people from collectivist cultures to communicate more assertively, while still maintaining a respectful and non-confrontational style. For instance, prefacing a question with "Excuse me, may I ask a question?" might seem unnecessary to some, but if it helps someone feel comfortable enough to engage, then it's entirely appropriate.

People with a more collectivist-influenced communication style can also learn to distinguish between situations. It is both appropriate and desirable to speak up assertively in contexts such as college or business settings, which can be differentiated from situations where culturally appropriate deference is preferred.

There is no single assertive communication style. Assertive communication can be adapted to fit cultural values and personal preferences.

Chapter 6
Becoming More Assertive

If being assertive were easy and natural for everyone, there wouldn't be so many books and workshops on the market aimed at improving assertiveness skills. However, whether you need a lot of improvement in this area or just a few adjustments, communication skills can be significantly improved through conscious effort. How we communicate is a highly modifiable skill that affects multiple important aspects of our lives, including our relationships, self-esteem, stress levels, and goal pursuits. This section will guide you through the basic steps of becoming more assertive or simply help you better understand the dynamics if you're already an effective communicator.

There are three basic steps to becoming more assertive:

146

- **Step One:** Learn your communication rights and the distinctions between passive, assertive, and aggressive communication.

- **Step Two:** Let this knowledge guide you in challenging negative thinking that interferes with assertiveness.

- **Step Three:** Get sufficient practice so that assertive communication becomes both habitual and comfortable.

You Have Rights

What people think can greatly influence what they do and how they do it. People can literally talk themselves out of speaking up assertively or into feeling angry and communicating aggressively. To begin reviewing how to challenge thinking that undermines assertive communication, consider whether you agree with the following statements:

People have basic rights that can be asserted:

- To agree or not
- To get what they pay for or what they were promised
- To set their own priorities and goals
- To put oneself first sometimes or in some circumstances
- To have and express one's own feelings and opinions
- To ask questions or ask for help
- To make mistakes or be undecided on occasion
- To change one's mind
- To postpone judgment or a decision if unsure
- To decide for oneself whether to accept help or advice
- To demand fair and respectful treatment
- To be taken seriously

Chances are, it was easy to agree with all the communication rights listed above, even if you do find it hard to speak up for yourself. On an intellectual level, most of us understand that someone has the right to say "no," change their mind, or hold an opinion different from others. However, a person might believe in these rights in a general sense without truly believing they apply to them personally.

People with lower self-esteem, for example, might struggle to believe that their personal opinions and feelings are just as valid as those of others. Because of negative thinking patterns, they may feel guilty about simply saying "no" or making a mistake. Likewise, someone might fear speaking up out of concern for looking foolish or being rejected, even though they intellectually understand that the feared outcome is unlikely.

149

Value Conflicts Make Communicating More Difficult

A person might hold the value that one should not disappoint or anger others, especially friends and family. While that may sound reasonable on the surface, we don't actually have that much control over how others feel. In addition, attempting *never* to upset anyone will inevitably come into conflict with valuing and standing up for our own rights and wishes.

What if someone you like solely as a workplace friend starts to develop a romantic crush on you and wants to start dating? Even if you say "no" very gently, is it still likely to disappoint that person? Yes. But what's the alternative? Making excuses or prioritizing their happiness over your own will backfire and make things worse for everyone.

The desire not to hurt other people's feelings is a positive value to hold, but it can also make it uncomfortable to give someone bad news. In many situations, the best we can do is be clear about our rights (to say "no," for example) and to express ourselves in a way that is both gentle and firm. In this example, you would tell your friend that you value the friendship and want it to continue, but do not want it to become more than that.

In addition, you can take a rational approach in how you think about the situation, something along the lines of: *"I'm sorry I had to disappoint him (or her), but there was no way around it. I handled it the right way. Occasional disappointments are part of life. I can't do any better than to be honest and sensitive."*

Challenge Negative Thinking

Knowing our communication rights helps us challenge negative thoughts that can interfere with communicating assertively. People often have all sorts of "What if?" thoughts running through their heads:

"What if I sound dumb?"

"What if this starts an argument?"

"What if they won't invite me to anything again if I say 'no' to this request?"

Negative thoughts like these can undermine a person's confidence and ability to speak up assertively. The steps to confronting negative thinking and shifting to a more positive inner dialogue, as reviewed earlier, can also be applied to thoughts that interfere with effective communication. Below are examples of how to reframe negative thoughts in ways that support assertive communication.

Challenge Negative Thinking:

Here are some examples of thoughts that inhibit effective communication alongside alternative thoughts that can help improve it.

Negative, Irrational Thoughts That Inhibit Effective Communication	Positive, Rational Thoughts That Facilitate Effective Communication
What if they get mad at me for disagreeing?	I have the right to my own opinion. I'll never know if people accept me for who I am if I don't show who I am. It's worth the risk.
What if I sound dumb?	People really aren't that critical, and I don't have to be perfect anyway. I'll never learn that it's safe to speak up if I don't try. I just need practice.
He/she didn't even call to let me know they'd be late! I can't believe what a selfish and thoughtless person they are. They won't be thoughtless when I get through with them.	I really don't like it when he/she doesn't call to let me know what's going on. Let me find out what happened and see if we can work out an agreement to avoid this sort of thing next time.

154

Practice Assertive Communication

It's not a guarantee, but assertive communication is generally well-received by most people in most situations. It works far better than passive or aggressive communication and is therefore more likely to be positively reinforced. Practicing assertive communication often leads to successful outcomes, which in turn makes it easier to challenge negative thinking in future situations. Positive thinking and assertive communication go hand in hand—each helps make the other stronger. The more people practice assertiveness, the easier and more natural both assertive communication and positive thinking become.

If being assertive is new to you, it may feel unnatural or uncomfortable at first. Begin by speaking up in easy situations, then try harder ones as you become more confident. Some situations are easier to speak up assertively than others, and these can serve as stepping stones to greater confidence and the ability to assert yourself in more complex situations.

To gain experience and build confidence, seize opportunities to speak up whenever possible and appropriate. If you've tended to be passive in the past, then practice is especially important. The more often you assert yourself and experience success, the easier assertive communication will become in the future.

Remember, becoming more assertive takes time and practice. It's also important to note that assertive communication comes in many styles. Assertiveness is not about finding the "perfect" words; there are many valid ways to express yourself assertively. You don't need to be perfect.

The goal is to shift out of passive or aggressive habits and develop a consistent, conscious practice of assertive communication.

How to Limit Conflict

Occasional interpersonal conflicts sometimes happen, and remaining assertive without slipping into passive or aggressive modes can be challenging at those times. Trying to avoid or eliminate all conflict is probably unrealistic and potentially harmful. Occasionally, conflicts can actually benefit a relationship by clearing the air and prompting one or both people to make positive changes. In addition, interpersonal conflicts can deepen the level of trust and commitment between people by demonstrating matter-of-factly that the relationship can tolerate disagreements, even hotly contested ones.

However, benefiting from conflicts is anything but a given. Interpersonal conflicts are a common cause of relationship dissatisfaction and breakups.

John Gottman is a leading researcher who studies what causes marriages to fail. He notes that what predicts future breakups is not whether couples argue, but how they argue. He identifies certain aggressive communication habits as particularly destructive. Beginning a discussion with unnecessarily harsh words or tone, for example. Also singled out as particularly harmful is criticizing someone's character. There is a big difference between complaining about a specific behavior or situation and criticizing the person's character. The latter is aggressive and more likely to damage the relationship.

158

In their self-help book *The Seven Principles for Making Marriage Work,* Gottman and Silver (1999) argue that showing disrespect for the other person and what they have to say is the most destructive communication habit in relationships. Sarcastic or cynical remarks such as *"Oh right, I forgot, you're perfect"* or *"Yeah, you're all talk"* convey contempt. Contempt can also be shown through name-calling, hostile humor, or mockery, as well as non-verbal cues such as sneers, laughs, smiles, and eye-rolling.

What appears predictive of marital breakup is a *pattern* of communication evident in how couples approach problems and disagreements. This should not be interpreted to mean that any slip into aggressive communication spells disaster for a relationship. Indeed, people who really care for and respect each other generally give one another a lot of slack. Healthy relationships are forgiving of slips and kinder in how they interpret each other's behavior. It is not the occasional slip-up, but a pattern of aggressive communication and negative interpretations that becomes increasingly predictive of relationship problems.

The difference between healthy and unhealthy relationships lies more in *how* and *how often* people argue than in whether they argue at all. In that regard, there are a number of communication strategies that can help decrease the frequency and intensity of conflicts. Here are some do's and don'ts to limit conflict.

"I" versus "You" Statements

Thinking through what we feel and want before discussing something serious can help make a two-way dialogue more effective.

Additionally, phrasing our comments and requests with *"I"* statements tends to elicit less defensiveness than *"you"* statements. *"I"* statements express what we think or feel about a behavior or situation and are followed by a specific request. If you're upset with a friend who consistently shows up late, you might say, "I'm not happy with the long waits. Can you be more realistic about the time you can actually make it?"

The essence of an *"I"* statement is that someone is expressing their own personal opinions without attacking the other person's character. While *"I"* statements can include complaints and potentially make the other person uncomfortable, they do not attack the person directly. They focus on situations and behaviors— things that can be changed and are less personal than criticisms of one's values or character.

Consequently, this approach tends to result in less defensiveness and more productive communication.

In contrast, the essence of a *"you"* statement is that it tends to attack the other person and put them on the defensive. Approaching the same tardy friend with the accusation, *"You are so inconsiderate! My time is important, and you don't seem to care!"* makes the message aggressive rather than assertive.

To be clear, it is the essence or overall tone of *"I"* versus *"you"* statements that matters, not merely whether the sentence starts with the word *"I"* or *"you."* For example, saying *"I think you're a slob"* still qualifies as a *"you"* statement in essence, even though it begins with *"I."* Aggressive communication, such as attacking someone with a

162

"you" statement, tends to lead to unproductive and hurtful interactions. Making valid complaints and requests for change using *"I"* statements increases the likelihood that the dialogue will be respectful and productive.

The following table shows examples of "I" versus "You" statements.

"You" Statement	"I" Statement
You don't care about our relationship or me. You could have called and let me know what was happening, but you only care about yourself.	I get really hurt and confused when you don't call and let me know that plans have changed. This pattern is going to have to stop. Can I get a commitment to change from you?
You haven't given me a raise since I started here six months ago. You don't appreciate what I do around here.	I've been working here for six months now and feel I'm doing a really good job. I'd like to discuss a salary increase.
You didn't follow your own grading guidelines. You gave me a "C" on this paper after I worked on it for two weeks.	I believe I followed your paper guidelines and wrote a good paper. I'd like to review with you how it was graded. I think it deserved more than a "C."

Set the Stage

Setting the stage for most discussions and assertive communications is unnecessary. Many situations don't require planning or scheduling. In fact, the (irrational) belief that we need to think through and plan out everything we are going to say can interfere with our ability to communicate in a spontaneous and natural way. Even serious discussions don't always need to be planned, as they can often happen naturally between people in any setting.

However, there are times when people want to talk about a subject matter in a way that sets the stage for a more productive conversation without distractions.

Trying to talk to someone when they are tired or obviously stressed increases the likelihood that the discussion won't go well. Setting the stage for a serious discussion can help reduce the risk of conflict by scheduling a time when both people are more likely to be relaxed, alert, and able to give each other their full attention.

A simple approach is to say, "I need to speak with you about **X**. Is this a good time?" Whether it is or not, this strategy tends to get the person's attention and sets the stage for a serious discussion. If the other person responds, "I'm in a hurry right now," it still leaves the door open to arrange a more convenient time. Either way, you have their attention.

You can use the simple idea of asking someone to talk as a way to start serious conversations with almost anyone about any topic. It is also helpful in getting someone out of the passive "wait" mode. Someone waiting for the perfect time or circumstance to ask someone out on a date or to ask a busy boss for a raise might end up waiting forever. By simply expressing your desire to talk about a subject, it doesn't have to be the perfect time, though you should still try to avoid obviously bad times.

Use Active Listening Skills

Some conflicts require nothing more than for the person doing the talking (the sender) to be listened to and understood. The use of active listening skills can go a long way toward preventing a dialogue from escalating into an argument. Of course, it's easier to stay in active listening mode if the sender is not being aggressive or attacking. However, even when being criticized or attacked, it is still possible to listen and try to understand the other person's viewpoint before responding. Active listening helps the receiver better understand the issue at hand, and it helps soothe the sender, a key element in conflict management.

Avoid Counter-Attacks

It has been said that the best defense is a good offense, but it depends on the ultimate goal. If your only goal is to gain the upper hand, counter-attacking might achieve that. On the other hand, if the real goal is to resolve a conflict and strengthen a relationship, counter-attacking is counterproductive.

Counter-attacking is generally easy to do. In fact, the better we know someone, the easier it is to counter-attack, precisely because we know their weaknesses. It takes a conscious awareness of the true goal, in this case, resolving a conflict and maintaining a positive relationship, to resist the temptation to counter-attack.

Stay Focused

It is easy for disagreements to expand beyond the issue at hand. What starts out as a discussion about arriving late can turn into an argument about friends, families, and personality traits. It is hard enough at times to resolve a single emotionally sensitive issue, let alone handle the chaos that arises when both parties bring in unrelated arguments to support their case. This significantly reduces the likelihood of a productive discussion.

Often, all it takes is one person to keep the discussion focused. When a conversation starts to stray into other issues, it can be reined in by either party saying, "Let's try to resolve just this one issue." This simple request may need to be repeated more than once.

Seek Compromise

Active listening and an open mind are essential to achieving compromise. If two people are unwilling to actively listen to each other or are not interested in working toward a mutually satisfying agreement, then compromise is unlikely. However, if they care about the relationship and want to find a way to resolve a conflict or impasse, seeking compromise can be effective.

Friends who want to go to different places for an outing might find an alternative place that both would like to visit. In other cases, it's not about finding a perfect middle ground, but about balancing needs so that both people feel the relationship is fair. One friend or partner might be unwilling to give up biking on Sunday mornings with friends, but may be willing to do other things their partner enjoys so that their partner's needs are also met.

Some issues do not have a workable middle ground. If one person wants to move across the country and the other wants to stay put, moving halfway won't satisfy either. In a healthy and equal relationship, one person will not always get everything their way. But through give and take, both individuals can hold on to what matters most to them while compromising on other things, helping the relationship feel fair to both parties.

Over the long term, relationships can maintain fairness through this kind of balance—one person gets their way sometimes, and the other gets theirs at other times. It doesn't have to be an exact 50/50 split or require keeping score. As long as both people feel it's fair, that's enough. The best that can be done is to understand and respect each other's positions and strive to make the relationship feel fair and equal over time. A long-term perspective and a willingness to give and take can help people move past even serious disagreements.

Postponing Discussion

Postponing a discussion can sometimes be necessary. Emotions can become so heightened that a rational and productive conversation is no longer possible. At such times, both parties may become focused on 'winning' the argument and slip into increasingly damaging attacks. In these situations, taking a break and cooling down is essential.

Different people also have varying tolerance levels for emotional intensity. One person may still be able to think clearly and want to finish a drawn-out and emotional discussion, while the other may be overwhelmed and unable to continue. Though it's not always the case, research suggests that men tend to reach their emotional limits more quickly than women. Gottman and Silver (1999) describe this as a person becoming "flooded," which often leads to them disengaging by "stonewalling" the other person.

Stonewalling is the act of appearing disinterested and unaffected by the other person's continued attempts to talk. A stonewaller may avoid eye contact, give no verbal or nonverbal feedback, and appear to focus on something else, such as reading a newspaper or watching TV. However, while someone stonewalling may appear undisturbed by what is going on, they are often greatly disturbed inside.

Gottman's research reveals that people who are feeling flooded show many signs of emotional overload, such as an extremely rapid heart rate, elevated blood pressure, and the release of stress hormones. To the person trying to continue the discussion, being stonewalled is also highly distressing. Based on their research, Gottman and Silver note that when verbal attacks create a pattern of flooding followed by a stonewalling defense within a marriage, it is predictive of divorce.

Fortunately, this pattern can be prevented. Active listening and non-aggressive communication can go a long way toward preventing either party from becoming emotionally overwhelmed (flooded) in the first place. However, maxing out emotionally can still happen, even within healthy relationships and communication patterns. People differ in their tolerance for conflict. When someone begins to max out during a drawn-out discussion or argument, it must be recognized and addressed through honest communication.

Unlike stonewalling, which is a one-sided and non-verbalized strategy, postponing discussion is a two-way communication. When either person reaches a point where they need to take a break, it must be verbalized openly. A person might say something along the lines of, "I know you want to finish this, but I can't think straight anymore. We need to continue this another time, after I've had time to think it through and can process what you're saying. Right now, I can't. I need to take a break."

The person who is able and willing to continue may not be happy about postponing the discussion, but it is far better than being stonewalled. Postponing an unproductive and heated discussion also offers the possibility that the issues may look entirely different the next day.

Consider two people who are tired and in a bad mood getting in an ugly argument over something trivial, like whose turn it is to load the dishwasher. In this situation, either person might recognize that things are getting out of hand and say, "Hey, this is getting out of hand. Let's drop it for now and talk about it tomorrow." The next day, when both parties are more rested, relaxed, and better able to put things in perspective, whose turn it was to do the dishes may seem pretty minor.

At that point, they might find themselves willing to compromise, or even apologize for their part in the disagreement.

Postponing discussion can be necessary at times and can help people step away from hurtful and unproductive conflicts, but it must be done with integrity.

Postponing is most likely to work when it is used honestly to express that someone is maxed out emotionally or that the situation needs time to cool down, not simply as an excuse to avoid a difficult conversation. In that regard, when an important discussion is postponed, it must be revisited. If one person asks to postpone a discussion but never wants to return to it, that's unlikely to sit well with the other person.

On the other hand, if friends, family members,

coworkers, or romantic partners learn that requests to postpone are sincere and do lead to follow-up conversations, the approach can work very well. This is true even when both parties later agree that the matter wasn't worth arguing about and choose to drop it. In fact, that's often a helpful and common outcome of postponing emotionally intense arguments over what are actually trivial concerns.

Additional Strategies for Conflict Management

- *Pick your fights.* Not every concern needs to be discussed, much less argued over.
- *Fight fair.* Name-calling, showing contempt for another's feelings or viewpoints, or deliberately saying what you know will hurt them only damages relationships.

- *Say you're sorry when appropriate and when you mean it.* Even if you weren't wrong about what you expressed, you might still be sorry for how you said it.

- *Keep promises you make, and if you can't, be honest.* Discuss why and see if the promise can be renegotiated.

- *Acknowledge positives* in the other person or in their perspective, rather than focusing only on the negatives.

- *Work on being a fair, reasonable person.* Build relationships with fair and reasonable people. It makes managing conflict much easier.

Chapter 7
Mental Health

Defining Mental Illness

Wouldn't it be horrible if, to be considered *normal*, we all had to act and think alike? Individual differences and preferences are part of what makes our society vibrant and healthy. But when does normal, healthy variability in emotions, behavior, and mental processes cross a threshold into symptoms of a mental disorder? It's not a simple question, but there are commonsense ways to approach an answer.

If someone has a habit of keeping junk around the house instead of throwing it away, is that a sign of mental illness? Let's hope not! But what if they keep so much junk that they can no longer sit in their living room or safely use their kitchen? That suggests something different.

If someone you know is sad and crying their

heart out, would you consider it a sign of mental illness? Would your opinion change depending on how long they had been feeling this way and whether something truly terrible had happened?

And what about a person who thinks they have a great singing voice, even if no one else agrees? Is that the same as someone believing aliens from outer space are controlling their thoughts?

The point at which normal variability in mental and behavioral functioning ends and abnormality begins is typically determined by assessing several criteria, as illustrated in the examples above. This is not unlike a medical evaluation, where lab results are compared against a normal range. Variability in emotions, behaviors, and mental processes can also be viewed within a range of what's considered typical. The criteria used by teams of health professionals to identify and classify mental disorders generally fall into four categories.

- Distress: A person is experiencing significant emotional distress that is disproportionate to, or cannot be explained by, their immediate circumstances. While acute sadness might be expected following the end of what had been a close relationship, thoughts of or attempts to end one's life would be considered an abnormal and disproportionate reaction. Likewise, occasional anxiety is normal, but feeling anxious and worried every day without a clear reason is not.

- A person's work or social functioning are significantly impaired due to psychological factors. Nervousness before a job interview or

182

on a first date is normal. However, if a person's anxiety is so overwhelming that they avoid dating or seeking better employment opportunities, this may indicate the presence of an anxiety disorder. When variability in emotional, behavioral, and mental processes reaches a level that significantly impairs normal functioning, it is more likely to be viewed as symptomatic of a mental disorder.

- A person may function outside the range of societal norms for acceptable behavior. For example, while talking out loud to oneself occasionally is relatively harmless and not uncommon, yelling loudly and aggressively in public with no one around is more likely to be seen as abnormal. Erratic patterns of emotion and behavior, or harming innocent people without experiencing guilt or anxiety, are additional examples of deviant behaviors that likely suggest the presence of a mental disorder.

- Gross disturbances in thought processes or in the ability to test reality, when not caused by temporary effects of drugs or a medical condition, also serve as key indicators. Hallucinations and delusions are especially prominent in this area. Hallucinations involve false sensory experiences, such as hearing voices when no one is present (auditory hallucinations), or seeing people or objects that are not there (visual hallucinations). A person's reality testing is further called into question when they hold fixed beliefs (called delusions) that clearly contradict reality. For instance, someone who believes they are constantly being spied on or plotted against, despite overwhelming evidence to the contrary, is likely experiencing paranoid delusions.

Using a combination of such criteria, along with analysis of a broad base of clinical research, teams of mental health professionals under the auspices of the American Psychiatric Association have developed the *Diagnostic and Statistical Manual of Mental Disorders* (DSM). This manual provides an empirical basis for identifying categories of mental disorders and the specific conditions that fall within each diagnostic category. The diagnosis of a particular condition is made based on the presence (or absence) of specific markers, allowing diverse professionals to reach more valid and reliable diagnostic conclusions.

While not perfect and still evolving, the use of this classification system has led to greater clarity and consistency in defining what does and does not constitute a specific mental disorder. DSM diagnoses and criteria are widely used not only by mental health professionals but also by other medical professionals and the insurance industry.

It's important to understand what having a mental health condition really means—and what it doesn't. Someone who meets the criteria for a DSM-defined mental disorder can still be kind, competent, and highly functional in both work and social roles, and this is often the case. Mental disorders, like many medical conditions, can be episodic rather than chronic, or affect only certain aspects of functioning.

Conversely, the absence of a mental disorder doesn't necessarily mean a person is happy, kind, or especially well-adjusted. People can be rude, inconsiderate, untrustworthy, obnoxious, foolish, or even a complete jerk, and still not meet the criteria for a specific diagnosis. The DSM and its definition of mental disorders don't cover everything.

Stress and Mental Illness

There are biological, psychological, and environmental factors involved in both physical and mental illness. So, it's perhaps no surprise that stress affects mental illness in much the same way it affects physical health. Stress can play a primary role in triggering a disorder, contribute to its onset, or make an existing condition worse. And just like with physical problems, the way stress impacts mental health depends on the severity and duration of the stress, as well as a person's coping abilities and personal vulnerabilities.

People with better coping skills and stronger

support systems tend to be more resilient. However, while coping skills can be learned and resources like social support can be developed, some factors are outside of our direct control.

Genetic variability also plays a role in mental illness, just as it does in physical health. Because of genetically based susceptibility, some people are more likely to develop a particular mental disorder than others. Early developmental influences beyond a child's control can also affect mental health in adulthood. For example, parental neglect and other forms of maltreatment have been shown to alter social functioning and brain chemistry in ways that increase susceptibility to anxiety and depressive disorders later in life.

Overall, various forms of mental illness represent a complex interaction between biological, psychological, and social factors, aptly referred to as the *interactionist perspective*. These three factors vary in their influence across different disorders. Some mental disorders are more biologically based, while others may be more influenced by psychological or social experiences. The influence of these factors also varies across different individuals with the same disorder. For example, one person's depression may be biologically caused, while another person's depression may be a reaction to recent events in their life.

Mental disorders also come in many types that range in severity, just like physical illnesses. Some mental disorders are chronic and disabling, but most are not. Many mental disorders can be short-lived episodes or involve symptoms that only arise under specific circumstances and do not significantly impact one's overall happiness or life functioning. Indeed, someone with a mental disorder may not just appear well-adjusted, but in fact be very happy and well-adjusted beyond those specific times and situations when their symptoms are active. I like to think that I'm an example of that. I was diagnosed with an anxiety disorder as a young man, but that hasn't stopped me from having a good, full life. Using the strategies reviewed in this book, I've been able to control my anxiety issues successfully.

Mental illnesses are not rare. They're common, with anxiety disorders and mood disorders being the most common. And just like with physical disorders, many mental disorders are highly treatable.

When Stress Management Isn't Enough

Psychologically healthy people may sometimes feel "stressed out." Feeling stressed is not by itself suggestive of a mental disorder, nor does having problems automatically mean someone needs professional mental health care. There are some mental and behavioral problems, though, that are so disruptive to a person's ability to function in work and social roles that the need for professional help becomes obvious. And there are other times when the need for professional help is not obvious, but would be helpful nonetheless.

A person doesn't need to be failing in an area of life to want help or simply gain insight. If someone feels stuck in their ability to clarify or improve an area of their life, even if they are not in great distress and are still functioning quite well in other aspects of life, it would still be completely reasonable to seek professional advice. Obtaining counseling services is a personal decision, and a person does not have to be experiencing a major crisis to do so. In fact, the various forms of therapy that are available can help prevent major problems from developing or help stop relatively minor problems from worsening.

There are some signposts, though, that would more clearly indicate the need for professional help. These include:

- Having thoughts of suicide or the desire to harm other people.
- Feeling unable to cope with normal demands.
- Abusing drugs, alcohol, or prescribed

medications to cope.

- Feeling powerless or hopeless to change in desired ways.

- Feeling chronically distressed (e.g., angry, anxious, or sad) and unable to pull out of it.

Types of Mental Health Treatments

Mental health care encompasses both inpatient and outpatient treatments, as well as personal counseling and medication management for mental and behavioral problems. Just like with medical issues, inpatient treatment is generally reserved for more urgent or disabling conditions that cannot be effectively treated on an outpatient basis. The vast majority of mental health care is delivered on an individual, outpatient basis and typically includes counseling, medication, or a combination of both.

It's also important to note that the term *therapy* is not limited to psychological interventions. It refers to any intervention that is soothing or curative. In the context of mental health care, *therapy* can refer to medication management just as readily as it can to talk therapies, often called *psychotherapy*.

Mental Health Providers

To independently assess and treat mental health problems, a provider must meet certain clinical training and licensing requirements. This training can be at the master's level, as with Licensed Clinical Social Workers (LCSWs) or Marriage and Family Therapists (MFTs). Psychologists must hold a doctoral degree (Ph.D., Psy.D., or Ed.D.) and also complete specific clinical training and licensing in order to assess and treat mental disorders. Psychiatrists, on the other hand, are medical doctors (M.D.s) who have completed a residency in psychiatry, rather than in general medicine, surgery, or another specialty.

All of these provider types can assess patient needs and provide psychotherapy. Psychiatrists, in particular, tend to treat more biologically based forms of mental illness, where medication management is often a primary approach. With very few exceptions, such as in certain military units, psychiatrists are the only mental health professionals authorized to prescribe medication.

Let's now take a closer look at psychotherapy and medication management.

What is Psychotherapy?

Psychotherapy is a professional relationship in

which a patient and therapist talk and work together to understand and treat one or more mental or behavioral problems the person is experiencing. Although mental health professionals vary in their training and the theoretical approaches they use, certain goals and characteristics are common to all effective psychotherapy interventions.

Major differences between providers typically emerge at the level of how they understand the causes of certain problems and how they believe those problems should be treated, based on their training and theoretical orientation.

The general goals and characteristics of psychotherapy can be summarized as follows:

- Informed consent is obtained. Fees, billing, cancellation policies, and confidentiality are discussed openly during the first visit. Clients are typically provided with written information about these policies.

- Legal and ethical guidelines are followed. All mental health providers must operate within their scope of training and adhere to professional ethical standards.

- Problems, goals, and diagnostic issues are clarified. Often within the first or second session, the therapist will clarify the client's presenting problems, treatment goals, and any relevant diagnosis or diagnoses. As with medical evaluations, some diagnostic issues take longer to clarify.

- A therapeutic alliance is developed. A foundation of rapport and trust between client and provider, along with provider credibility, is an important part of therapy. This alliance is usually established early in the process, and is critical for effective ongoing treatment.

- Background is reviewed, and antecedent factors are identified. Providers work to understand what factors may have triggered the client's current symptoms or difficulties. They also gather background information such as family and work history, prior mental health care, and substance use in order to better understand the client's situation and how best to help them.

- A treatment plan is adopted. This is the stage where differences in therapeutic orientation and approach become most apparent.

Types of Psychotherapy

Once a client's problems and background are sufficiently understood, a therapist is in a position to discuss their impressions and treatment recommendations with the client. Psychotherapy involves a treatment plan that reflects the information gathered and the goals identified. However, the treatment plan will vary depending on the therapist's theoretical orientation.

Although long-term psychotherapy lasting several years is still a respected option for certain problems and goals, briefer and more problem-focused treatments have become the norm. Many mental health issues can often be successfully addressed over the course of months rather than years. The psychotherapeutic process today is far less mysterious and drawn-out than it was in the early days of Freudian psychoanalysis, and generally more successful.

Psychodynamic Therapy

Sigmund Freud, in the early 1900s, developed comprehensive theories of personality development and psychopathology. He is often referred to as the "Father of Psychology," though many of his original theoretical ideas are either unsubstantiated or have been disproven over time.

Freudian-based psychoanalysis is still practiced, but it is far less common than more modern psychodynamic approaches. Some newer psychodynamic therapies retain some core Freudian principles, such as the importance of unconscious processes and dreams, as well as the importance of developmental conflicts in understanding and treating what they view as deeper character structures.

However, these psychodynamic therapists

tend to play a more active, collaborative role in therapy than the Freudian approach to psychoanalysis. They sit facing the patient and are more talkative and emotionally expressive. Feelings and experiences that show themselves within the context of the therapy session are now commonly used to enrich psychodynamic therapy.

Current forms of psychodynamic therapy have also become more theoretically diverse, reflecting influences from various schools of thought. The field is alive with debate about what actually generates the changes seen in therapy. The time frame and frequency of sessions have also become much more varied among psychodynamic therapists, including the practice of shorter-term, symptom-focused therapy.

However, while psychodynamic therapy

remains a popular and effective form of intervention, cognitive-behavioral therapy (CBT) has been found superior in most studies on treatment effectiveness, especially for some of the most common disorders such as depression and anxiety, as well as in many areas of health and health behavior management.

Before discussing CBT, I should mention that I was trained in a university-based doctoral program in clinical psychology with a cognitive-behavioral and social learning theory orientation. I also ran a CBT-based clinical practice for 25 years, so this is an area where I'm especially knowledgeable—and admittedly, a bit biased.

Cognitive-Behavioral Psychotherapy

As the name implies, Cognitive-Behavioral Therapy (CBT) integrates both cognitive and behaviorally based interventions. CBT has risen in popularity due to its proven clinical effectiveness across a wide range of common disorders, as well as its cost-effectiveness.

In practice, therapists working from a CBT model use and combine a variety of specific interventions tailored to a client's symptoms and treatment goals. While the interventions may sound educational in nature, they are always delivered within the context of a therapeutic relationship and a deep understanding of the client's concerns. Just as with other types of therapy, CBT involves a great deal of careful listening and emotional support.

Primary examples of intervention strategies that fall within the scope of CBT are outlined below:

- *Cognitive Therapy:* The basic strategy of the cognitive component of CBT is to help clients recognize and shift out of distorted and overly negative thinking and beliefs that affect their feelings, decisions, and behavior. Within the context of a supportive professional relationship, the therapist provides theoretically based expertise to help patients recognize and change maladaptive thoughts and beliefs.

- *Exposure-Based Treatments:* Exposure-based treatments use the natural process of habituation to overcome a variety of fears. One example of an exposure-based approach is called *Systematic Desensitization,* a step-by-step intervention originally developed by Joseph Wolpe (1958) for extinguishing maladaptive responses to feared situations.

204

It is this repeated exposure, at tolerable levels of anxiety, that produces habituation, resulting in a decreased fear response. Through a combination of both imagining and practicing successful steps toward overcoming a feared stimulus, the person adapts and begins to respond with less fear. Exposure-based interventions are successfully used to help clients overcome a number of anxiety-related conditions.

For example, a person who is terrified of dogs might first watch puppies in a kennel until it elicits little anxiety, then stand next to the puppy cage, then stand next to someone holding a puppy, then near someone with a mellow, old dog, and so on. By working through a hierarchy of fear-producing situations, the person is gradually "desensitized" to achieve a desired level of comfort. In this case, a person with a dog phobia might continue desensitization until they can be around friendly dogs in people's homes or walk comfortably past dogs on the street.

- *Skill Development and Behavior Change:* Though an emphasis on social skills training and relationship difficulties is sometimes labeled *interpersonal therapy* or *social skills training*, social skills development is a common component of CBT. Assertive communication, for example, is often taught within the context of CBT.

  Other behavioral goals commonly addressed in CBT include helping patients develop relaxation techniques, parenting skills, time management, goal setting and problem-solving skills, better habit control, reducing procrastination, improving sleep routine, or learning how to better manage medical problems such as chronic pain.

The essence of behavior therapies is to help people identify and decrease unwanted behaviors, thoughts, and emotional reactions, while identifying and increasing desired responses. These behavioral goals are integrated with and supported by the cognitive interventions described above.

Clients receiving CBT are also sometimes given directive behavioral 'prescriptions,' such as to increase their planning for use of leisure time, social involvement, or exercise to further improve mood and bring more balance into their lives.

Other Approaches

Individual psychotherapy is the most widely

used form of psychotherapeutic intervention. However, personal growth retreats, as well as group, family, and couples' therapies, are also available and commonly used. Like individual psychotherapy, these approaches vary in their theoretical foundations, with psychodynamic, supportive, and cognitive-behavioral models being the most dominant.

Couples and family therapies provide the most direct intervention for resolving problems that exist within relationships. Group psychotherapy sacrifices some of the individualized attention and privacy found in one-on-one treatment but offers unique advantages over individual treatment for certain issues and challenges.

Group, couples, and family treatments can also be provided alongside individual counseling,

208

though typically not by the same mental health provider. Just as a medical doctor might follow a patient for a back injury, prescribe medication, and refer the patient to physical therapy, psychological therapies can also be combined. In fact, psychotherapy and medication management are commonly used together.

Medication Management

Both physiological and psychological factors are important in understanding and treating mental disorders. In general, the more biologically driven a disorder is, the more likely it is that medications will be helpful for effective treatment. As mentioned earlier, some mental disorders have a stronger biological basis than others. Schizophrenia, for example, is one of the more biologically based disorders, with a strong genetic component. It is also among the more serious and chronic mental health conditions, affecting about 1% of the general population.

Before the advent of antipsychotic medications, the hallucinations and delusions associated with schizophrenia were virtually untreatable, and individuals with the disorder often required institutional care. Since then, many pharmacological advancements have been made. Still, almost all mental disorders can be best understood as resulting from an interaction between psychological and biological factors. As with medical conditions, medications can be beneficial for a wide range of mental health issues.

The question of whether or not to use medication is largely based on an analysis of risks and benefits, and that holds true whether the problem is medical or psychological. Even a simple aspirin regimen can cause serious, unwanted side effects in some individuals. Psychoactive medications are no different in that regard. However, the stigma around mental illness and widespread misinformation about what psychoactive medications do may cause more people to be wary of them than of other prescriptions.

That said, there are many psychoactive medications that are considered safe and effective. The bottom line is whether the potential benefits justify the use of a medication that carries certain possible side effects or risks.

In many cases, the answer to whether or not to use medication is clearly yes. Some mental disorders are so disabling and biologically based that the potential benefit of medication use clearly outweighs the risks. In other cases, symptoms may not be as severe or as biologically rooted, making medication less necessary or appropriate.

Still, medications are not a cure-all. They don't work for everyone. They can have side effects ranging from mild to serious, and some carry concerns about dependency. In some cases, they may be used or prescribed even when non-pharmacological approaches would be more effective. However, none of these concerns are unique to psychoactive medications.

The problem with medication treatment is not the medications themselves, but the potential for overuse and misuse, just like with any other prescription or over-the-counter drug. Many mental disorders are successfully treated without any medication at all. That said, when psychoactive medications are used and tolerated in the right amount and for the right reasons, the benefits can outweigh the risks, and in many cases, those risks are minimal.

Medications and Psychotherapy

Both medication and psychotherapy have been found to be effective in the treatment of mental disorders when used as standalone approaches. However, medications by themselves don't help people gain insight into their problems and patterns or teach new coping skills. In fact, medication management may not even be appropriate for many types of stress-related problems, where the more effective approach is to reduce the source of stress or improve coping abilities rather than simply medicate away the symptoms.

Unlike medication, psychotherapy helps people gain insight, develop skills, and support positive life changes. Because of this, psychotherapy alone can sometimes be more effective than medication in the long run for treating common emotional and behavioral problems.

When psychotherapy or medication management are not sufficient as singular approaches, the ideal approach often becomes a combination of both—psychotherapeutic intervention plus medication management. These are distinct but complementary treatments that, when used together as indicated, can offer optimal outcomes.

214

Getting Professional Help

Roadblocks to mental health care remain substantial. Studies suggest that in our society, less than half of the people with a mental disorder receive professional mental health care. And for those who do seek care, there is often a delay of ten years or more before treatment is obtained.

Unmet treatment needs are most prevalent among people who are poor, have less education, live in rural communities, or belong to minority groups. While available evidence suggests that the stigma surrounding mental illness and its treatment has lessened over time, it is far from gone.

Mental illness is extremely common and costly, both in terms of human suffering and lost productivity, yet it continues to be misunderstood and under-treated. Clearly, more work is needed to both educate the public about mental health and the effective treatments available and to remove the significant financial and accessibility barriers to obtaining mental health care. These barriers are real and substantial.

For More Information

- **Centers for Disease Control and Prevention (CDC):**

  The CDC offers information and recommendations on suicide prevention and other health topics at:

- www.cdc.gov/ncipc/dvp/suicide

- **National Institute of Mental Health (NIMH):**

  NIMH provides easy-to-read articles and fact sheets on a wide range of mental health topics at:

www.nimh.nih.gov/health/publications/index.shtml

- **The Surgeon General's Report on Mental Health:**

  This report offers a broad, accessible overview of mental health issues in the U.S. It can be reviewed or ordered for free at:

  www.surgeongeneral.gov/library/mentalhealth/

Chapter 8
Successful Aging

While on faculty in the Department of Medicine at UCSF Medical Center in 1990, I was lead author on a workbook for successful aging. It was produced under a grant by the Office of Prevention of the California Department of Mental Health. Titled *Aged to Perfection: Your Guide to Healthy Aging*, it provided readers with guidance on how to improve health as we age, along with practical tools and information for addressing common challenges of aging.

At the heart of successful aging is quality of life, not just physical health, and certainly not just longevity. The workbook explained that how we choose to live our lives and deal with challenges matters *twice as much* as our genes when it comes to how we age. On a population basis, our daily habits and attitudes have a much bigger impact on aging than what we inherit from our parents. Despite being written over 35 years ago, the most basic and powerful recommendations for healthy living have changed very little.

In their landmark review, Drs. Rowe and Kahn (1987) contrasted successful aging with the more typical declines associated with growing older. Differences in how people age can be dramatic. Some individuals in their 70s, 80s, and into their 90s remain vibrant and healthy, while others in their 50s struggle to walk a single block uphill without stopping to rest. There is variability in health and functioning among children and young adults as well, of course, but the differences become much more pronounced in middle and old age.

With the advances we've made in public health

measures affecting the safety of our food, water, air, and sanitation, and breakthroughs in medical care, particularly developments in antibiotics and vaccines, people today live much longer on average than in the past. However, with more people reaching advanced age comes the accumulated wear and tear on the body, and with it a higher risk of developing chronic, lifestyle-related diseases. Heart disease, cancer, stroke, Alzheimer's disease, arthritis, emphysema, and many other conditions become more common in old age because they typically take decades to develop.

But major health problems in old age are not inevitable. We can greatly influence our future health and well-being by adopting a healthier lifestyle. Our day-to-day health habits are the most important factor in how we age. Unfortunately, many people learn about preventive health care in scattered bits and pieces from various sources. This information can be confusing and may not appear to fit together well. That can negatively affect motivation.

The most basic and powerful recommendations for maintaining good health actually fit and work well together. In many cases, they overlap. By making a few clear and simple choices, you can seriously boost your chances of living a healthier and more fulfilling life.

Healthy living isn't all or nothing, and you're never too old to get started. An excellent example of this is the research of Fiatarone, et.al., (1994) and Binder, et.al., (2005) showing that exercise interventions, when done safely and correctly can significantly improve strength and mobility, even in the most frail of very elderly people. We're never too old to benefit from positive changes in our health habits.

About the Exceptions

Everybody knows about the exceptions, which, by definition, stand out. Are there occasions where health-conscious, active people die of a heart attack at a relatively young age? Yes. Are there people who smoke and drink heavily for decades yet remain in reasonably good health well into old age? Yes. But in both cases, these are true exceptions to the norm. Good health habits don't offer a guarantee, but they do shift the odds in our favor considerably.

Shifting the odds is how most areas of our lives work. Few, if any, long-term goals come with ironclad guarantees. Being a good parent doesn't guarantee that our children will grow into happy, successful adults, but it certainly improves the odds. There are exceptions to the rule in nearly everything, but that doesn't lead people to discount the value of being a good parent, and it shouldn't lead anyone to devalue the importance of good health habits either.

There are some less common diseases, like hemophilia and cystic fibrosis, that are entirely genetically determined. Also, if your goal is to live past 100, having many long-lived relatives will improve your chances, since maximum lifespan is largely genetically set. However, whether or not you reach your genetic maximum age, and in what condition, is most heavily influenced by your lifestyle.

For the vast majority of people, when it comes

to the most common major health problems and aging goals, like staying healthy, independent, and fulfilled into advanced age, heredity plays a relatively minor role compared to lifestyle influences on a population level.

Now, this doesn't mean hereditary influences should be ignored—far from it. On an individual basis, they are important. A family history of a particular disease can increase someone's risk of developing that same condition. However, it's also important to understand that, for the most common causes of death and disability, such as heart disease, cancer, and stroke, what's inherited is not the disease itself, but a combination of genetic factors that can increase or decrease susceptibility.

Whether these genetic predispositions

develop into actual disease is largely influenced by lifestyle and the precautions a person takes or doesn't take. Studies of identical twins have found that even when both die from the same disease, the age at which it happens can vary widely due to lifestyle differences. In fact, because of those differences, it's not only possible, but quite common, for a disease to appear in one twin and not in the other, despite their identical genetic makeup.

Here's how your lifestyle can affect the health risks you inherit from your family. An easy example is someone who inherits a much higher-than-normal sensitivity to the cancer-causing substances in cigarette smoke. Because of their inherited susceptibility, if they smoke, they're almost certain to develop smoking-related cancer. However, despite that genetically based susceptibility, if they don't smoke and aren't regularly exposed to secondhand smoke, they can avoid that outcome.

Another example is someone with a strong family history of early-onset heart disease. They don't inherit heart disease. They might, though, inherit a genetically based predisposition toward high cholesterol, high blood pressure, and heightened sodium sensitivity, which are factors that greatly increase their risk for heart disease and stroke. But with a healthy diet that includes adequate sodium restriction, regular exercise, weight control, and the use of blood pressure or cholesterol-lowering medications when needed, their inherited risk can be significantly reduced.

Lifestyle and medical management don't change a person's genetic makeup, but they can often do the next best thing: neutralize or prevent a genetically influenced problem from developing. That's why, when a family history places someone at increased risk for a health problem, both medical and lifestyle management become even more important.

Common Causes of Death and Disability

Heart disease, cancer, and stroke have become leading causes of death since the development of antibiotics and vaccines. Before that, infectious diseases were the primary killers. Now, the leading causes of death are largely degenerative diseases that take years to develop. Other common causes of death and disability in old age include dementia (most often Alzheimer's disease), peripheral vascular disease, accidents, type 2 diabetes, emphysema, cirrhosis of the liver, osteoporosis, osteoarthritis, chronic back pain, and loss of mobility due to fear, weakness, or imbalance. All of these conditions (with the exception of accidents) share a common feature: they typically develop over long periods of time and are heavily influenced by lifestyle factors.

Changes in our bodies caused by poor lifestyle habits, like lack of exercise or unhealthy eating, often happen so slowly that we mistake these accumulated changes from lifestyle habits for normal aging. While some decline in strength, fitness, and energy is inevitable with age, many of the changes commonly seen in old age are neither natural nor inevitable.

When someone 'suddenly' has a heart attack, what usually has gone unnoticed are the many years of gradual buildup of fatty plaque in the arteries supplying blood to the heart. Likewise, when someone's back 'suddenly' goes out, it's usually the result of years of unnoticed degenerative changes and physical deconditioning.

Cellular changes that lead to cancer also develop silently over many years. In fact, the majority of cancers are linked to lifestyle factors such as smoking, excessive sun exposure, and poor dietary habits, including alcohol abuse. Accidents are also a common cause of death and disability in old age. But even traumatic injuries, such as those caused by falls, are influenced by one's health habits. Why? Because people who keep in good physical condition are less likely to fall in the first place, less likely to suffer serious injury if they do fall, and more likely to recover fully if they are injured. The goal of preventive health care is to slow down, or avoid entirely, the degenerative processes that lead to many common health problems.

Do Health Experts Agree?

Health experts who follow the science and data agree almost unanimously on core health recommendations. Minor controversies and disagreements may arise when fine-tuning these core recommendations for specific health problems or in determining the extent to which a particular health habit relates to a specific disease. So yes, you can find disagreements about which exercise routine is best or which protein sources are preferable. But you won't find disagreement about the basics. This leaves plenty of flexibility to adopt health behaviors that suit your cultural and personal preferences.

Health habits tend to affect more than one health goal at a time. In fact, most health habits influence many health goals simultaneously, and that's a good thing! This means you don't have to remember, let alone follow, a completely different set of rules depending on your particular goals.

Look online at healthy dietary recommendations from reputable sources such as the WHO, NIH, CDC, and the Dietary Guidelines for Americans. With extremely slight variations, they all say essentially the same thing: a healthy, balanced diet is low in saturated fats, sodium, and added sugars; high in whole grains, fruits, and vegetables; includes adequate healthy protein sources; and emphasizes portion control.

When healthy dietary practices become the day-to-day norm, the occasional celebration or break from routine becomes inconsequential. Life is meant to be enjoyed, and food and celebrations are a part of that. It's not the occasional birthday cake or fast-food lunch that causes harm. Rather, it's the daily eating habits that affect us the most.

Unfortunately, recent studies reported by the CDC in August 2025 found that ultra-processed foods (unhealthy choices) make up more than 50% of Americans' calories, contributing to higher rates of obesity, diabetes, and cardiovascular disease.

Ultra-processed foods, which often combine high levels of sugars, sodium, refined carbs, and unhealthy fats, may taste great, but they're designed to appeal to our taste buds rather than meet our nutritional needs. They're also widely available, heavily marketed, and highly convenient—all of which make them especially easy to overindulge in.

In line with healthy dietary recommendations, the CDC encourages people to greatly limit these foods, which contain little to no whole ingredients, are low in dietary fiber, and are often loaded with salt, sweeteners, and unhealthy fats. Examples include most candy bars, sugar-sweetened beverages, fast-food meals and snacks, and many breakfast cereals.

Whether your goal is to limit excess weight gain or reduce the risk of heart disease, cancer, stroke, obesity, high blood pressure, diabetes, and more, the same healthy diet is recommended. You can tweak it slightly for specific goals, such as emphasizing calorie control more for weight loss, but the core recommendations remain the same.

The vast number of fad diets that lead to weight loss usually result in only short-term success, with approximately 95% of those who lose weight on fad diets gaining it back. The key is long-term consistency, which generally requires finding healthier foods and meal preparation methods that you actually enjoy. No one has to twist our arm to eat foods that taste really good when we're hungry. And, as previously mentioned, keeping temptations, those far less healthy options, out of the house helps too. In fact, replacing just a couple of poor choices you make regularly with healthier alternatives can make a huge difference over time.

Getting regular, sufficient exercise is another mainstay of wellness. Like healthy eating, it supports many health and wellness goals simultaneously. Just half an hour of well-targeted stretching and strengthening exercises twice a week, along with regular, sustained aerobic activities that elevate your heart rate can reduce the risk of heart disease, stroke, high blood pressure, diabetes, obesity, insomnia, cognitive decline, and problems with balance and stability, while also helping to lower stress and improve mood. Healthy eating and regular exercise pair perfectly and powerfully.

As with healthy eating, finding ways to get sufficient exercise that you ideally enjoy, or at least won't avoid, is key. Starting or maintaining a healthier lifestyle long-term is the goal. If someone is not currently maintaining a sufficiently active lifestyle, starting out with gradual increments is less likely to result in frustration or setbacks, especially if the person is elderly or frail. Simply increasing the length of your walks by five minutes each week can potentially build up to one-hour walks within a few months.

Your health care providers should be able to offer guidance on how to start exercising more safely, as well as recommend where to find reliable exercise information and instructions. Here, too, a bit of self-knowledge goes a long way. Finding the types of exercise and ways of exercising that work best for you personally increases the likelihood that you will stick with them. You don't want to be one of the many people who buy exercise equipment that ends up being used as a coat rack. Besides, exercise equipment is an option, not a requirement. Even something as simple as regular long walks is a great form of exercise… and when it's paired with socializing or time in nature, it has even broader benefits.

Staying aware of the many lifestyle choices that affect our health and quality of life allows us to prioritize and balance our lives more effectively. It helps us avoid getting bogged down in the details or becoming overly focused on one thing while neglecting something else of equal or greater importance. A healthy, balanced lifestyle actually incorporates much of what represents "the good life": satisfying relationships, eating well, taking time to relax and enjoy ourselves, being physically active, mentally engaged, and meaningfully involved in life.

Below are Ten Keys to Health and Wellness

✓ **Get Regular Medical Checkups:** Many unhealthy changes in body function can progress without noticeable symptoms. Detecting increases in blood pressure, cholesterol, and blood sugar, for example, allows people to take action before these issues develop into heart disease or diabetes. Follow your doctor's guidance regarding exams, lab tests, immunizations, cancer screens, and managing personal risk factors. Early detection saves lives. Irregularities that are caught early generally provide more and better options for intervention. Medical care combined with positive personal health habits form the perfect partnership for preventive health care and successful aging.

✓ **Take Good Care of Your Oral Health:** Our oral health doesn't just affect our ability to properly chew; it also affects our overall health and has been linked to cardiovascular disease in particular. Follow your dentist's advice regarding check-ups and daily oral hygiene.

✓ **<u>Stay Socially Involved and Connected:</u>** The quality and frequency of our relationships are not only the best predictors of life satisfaction, but also strongly linked to our mental and physical health. Social connections fulfill a basic human need and require regular contact with people we genuinely care about, and who care about us in return.

✓ **<u>Stay Mentally Active and Meaningfully Involved in Life:</u>** Disuse doesn't just affect your muscles; we also need to keep exercising our minds and expressing our values. Goals and activities that align with our interests and values take on meaning. We need to use our minds and stay engaged with what matters to us. Leisure activities that offer opportunities to socialize and problem-solve provide more than just enjoyment. To thrive, we need reasons to get out of bed: things we need to do, things we want to do, and things to look forward to.

✓ **Stay Physically Active:** Purposeful exercise is great, but at a minimum, you should regularly engage in a variety of activities that get you up and moving for extended periods, ideally doing things you find naturally enjoyable. See the exercise recommendations reviewed earlier in this chapter, as well as guidance from your health care providers and sources like the NIH.

✓ **Develop Healthy Eating Habits:** It's your normal, day-to-day eating habits that make the biggest difference. A diet low in saturated fats, added sugars, and sodium, and high in fruits, vegetables, and whole grains—with adequate protein and moderate calorie intake—leaves plenty of room for personal preferences. Finding healthy food choices and recipes you enjoy makes it much easier to stick with your healthy eating habits and sustain them over time.

✓ **<u>Develop Good Coping Skills to Manage Stress:</u>** As reviewed in previous chapters, developing positive thinking habits, effective communication skills, and positive social connections are key strategies for managing stress. Exercise, active problem solving, enjoying leisure outlets, and doing something positive for yourself or for others are additional ways to reduce and buffer stress. And just as we seek professional help for medical concerns, professional mental health care is also available and valuable.

✓ **Use Good Safety Practices:** Falls and many other accidents can often be avoided by the simple combination of using good judgment and taking precautions. Removing trip hazards, anticipating risks, driving defensibly, and using sunscreen are examples of ways to reduce common risks. Using proper body mechanics when bending, sitting, or lifting heavy objects is an additional example of simple choices that help avoid injury.

✓ **Give Yourself Adequate Sleep and Rest:** Specific sleep needs vary, but most people require about eight hours of sleep per day. Getting sufficient exercise during the day, combined with a regular sleep routine, managing stress, and avoiding alcohol or caffeine in the evening are basic strategies for improved sleep.

✓ **Avoid Substance Abuse:** Avoid entirely the abuse of drugs, including medications. Alcohol is also a drug with addictive potential, and no one recommends that anyone start drinking alcohol. Even moderate consumption can pose health risks. That said, alcohol is commonly consumed by many millions of people. The CDC and the 2020 – 2025 Dietary Guidelines for Americans recommend that if you do drink alcohol, then do so responsibly and in moderation. Moderate alcohol intake is defined as being no more than two drinks per day for men, and no more than one drink per day for women. A single drink is one 12-oz beer, or one 5-oz glass of wine, or 1.5 oz of distilled spirits.

Cigarette smoking should be avoided entirely, as it is the leading preventable cause of disease and death in the United States. The U.S. Food and Drug Administration (fda.gov) notes that no tobacco use is safe, but that tobacco that is smoked, as are cigarettes, releases more toxins and is most harmful. According to the Centers for Disease Control and Prevention (cdc.gov), smoking and second-hand exposure harms nearly every organ in the body, and is the cause of nearly half a million deaths in the U.S. each year.

Chapter 9
End-of-Life

Some loss of physical functioning and vitality as we grow older is inevitable. The average person, however, begins to decline in early middle age far more rapidly than aging alone would account for. The attainable ideal is for people to experience only a modest decline until they reach their genetically determined maximum age, at which point a rapid deterioration is often seen and leads to death. We all die. This is as good as it gets: leading a full, active life right up until the end of advanced old age.

But for most people, things don't go that way. They lose more ability than they need to, and the loss of vitality and independence in old age can span many years. With an aging population, the demand for home care, assisted living facilities, memory care units, and nursing homes continues to grow.

While filling an obvious need, end-of-life care and decisions are both practically and emotionally complicated. Decisions about the timing, type, and level of care needed, finding the right caregivers or facilities, and making these transitions—all of it is complicated. On top of that, long-term care is expensive and not generally covered by health insurance.

I have visited several assisted living facilities, including frequent visits to a pricey memory care unit where my brother resided. It had a huge, beautifully landscaped courtyard with well-placed benches and picnic tables. Despite open access, I rarely saw any of the residents out there—usually none at all. Mostly, I saw people sitting inside— some with blank stares, others sitting or pacing with anxious, fearful expressions. But there were also residents socializing who seemed content enough. Speaking just for myself, none of the facilities I visited are places I would ever want to be in. But life doesn't always offer people better choices.

Alzheimer's disease is the leading cause of dementia in old age, and a common cause of death and disability. Alzheimer's disease is a condition of the brain marked by the slow buildup of amyloid plaques and tau tangles, which increasingly compromise cognitive function and leads to progressive dementia. The causes of Alzheimer's are still not fully understood but appear to involve a complex interaction of genetic, lifestyle, and environmental factors. Age is by far the greatest risk factor, with the vast majority of cases occurring in individuals over the age of 65.

In its advanced stages, Alzheimer's can be

completely debilitating, yet people often live with it for many years. It can be a cruel disease, both for those who suffer from it and for their loved ones. I know this from personal experience, and I have come to hold strong opinions about how our society addresses end-of-life care and the choices we have around it.

All three of my much older siblings—13, 19, and 21 years older than me—were diagnosed with Alzheimer's and died after years of pointless suffering and disability. I told my primary care physician that I would want to end my own life if I had clearly started down that same path and asked if I would be able to get a prescription for a tried-and-true barbiturate for that purpose. He replied, "Absolutely not. I'm not going to prescribe you something to kill yourself with."

It was a dumb question to pose to my physician, with such an expected response. It's far from a dumb question, though. End-of-life care and options are serious and complicated issues that need discussion. We will start with pets.

When our now-grown son was four years old, my wife and I got him a puppy so he could grow up with a dog to love and care for. We named the pup Cory, and he quickly became a beloved member of our family. Cory was a sweet, gentle dog who slept in our son's bedroom, joined us on hikes, and curled up in the living room while we watched TV. Cory was loved.

The love we often feel for our pets is the real thing. We care deeply about their well-being and happiness. We look after them in sickness and in health. And we can deeply mourn their passing.

It's true love. And when their health irreversibly deteriorates to the point where we can see them needlessly suffering, our love can often lead us to end their suffering. Many pet owners choose euthanasia as a humane and loving alternative to prolonged pain and suffering.

That's what happened with Cory. By the time he was 14, his respiratory and arthritic problems were so severe that he could barely walk. Watching Cory struggle to stand after he had been lying down made us cringe. Cory was suffering. It was a sad time and situation. The humane society that helped us put Cory down handled everything with kindness and understanding. We loved Cory, and it was an incredibly difficult decision, but the right one. It was a caring, dignified, and merciful end to his life.

In contrast, end-of-life issues for us humans are far more complicated, and sometimes, far less humane and dignified. Obviously, we're not like pets. No one wants another person to have the power to arbitrarily decide when we're better off dead. The one widely accepted exception is in cases of an irreversible and complete vegetative state (i.e., brain death), where the difficult decision to withdraw or withhold life support may be made.

Outside of that, however, people have very limited legal options when it comes to making their own end-of-life choices. As a result, it's not uncommon for individuals to live on, sometimes for many years, despite enduring obvious suffering, with no quality of life and no hope of improvement. My much older brother Bill's final years are a case in point, and sadly, not an unusual one.

By the time Bill was formally diagnosed with Alzheimer's, he was no longer the man we knew. Once an avid outdoorsman and lifelong sports enthusiast, he lost interest in everything he used to love. He could no longer function independently and needed help with the most basic tasks. He was constantly confused, often anxious and agitated, and had lost bowel control. Yet he had years more of life ahead of him, and a prognosis that said his condition would only worsen. And it did.

Bill was a good person, and this was a hell of a way for his life to end. Bill's loving wife, along with all of us who cared, were powerless and anguished passengers on this journey too. Cory received a much more humane and dignified end to his life than my brother and countless others like my brother.

254

Current advanced medical directives can limit the level of intervention used in a medical emergency, such as ensuring a patient is not resuscitated against their wishes. Other voluntary medical directives allow patients to specify how much life-sustaining treatment they want if they become seriously ill. Patients also have the right to decline further treatment or specific interventions, such as surgery or chemotherapy. In some states, people with a medically documented terminal illness may request physician-assisted suicide as an option.

I personally believe that freedom of choice in these situations is a good start, yet it doesn't address or help countless end-of-life issues, such as the one my brother faced. He had an advance directive, but never had a life-threatening emergency that required resuscitation or life support. And if he had the mental wherewithal (which he did not) and lived in a state that allowed medically assisted suicide, he still wouldn't have qualified. His condition was progressive and irreversible, but not terminal in any short-term sense. People diagnosed with Alzheimer's can live for years—even decades.

For personal and legitimate reasons, many, perhaps even the vast majority of people facing irreversible and devastating declines in their physical or cognitive abilities, would choose to live out their remaining years. That is their right, and depending on their personal beliefs, values, and family circumstances, it may be the absolutely right choice for them. But it is not the right or desirable choice for everyone. It is not how I want to spend my final years. When the evidence and prognosis are clear, I believe that anyone facing irreversible loss of independence, severe decline in quality of life, and prolonged suffering should have the right to end their life on their own terms, if that is what they choose.

Not all suicides are irrational acts of desperation. I should know, and I do! I was a practicing clinical psychologist for 25 years. Not just depression, but a number of mental disorders are associated with an increased risk of suicide. Assessment and management of suicide risk were integral parts of my practice. Suicidal ideation or intent in someone who is in emotional distress and temporarily unable to see or believe that things can improve must always be taken seriously. And I intervened successfully many times in my 25-year practice.

However, if we can conclude that it's

inhumane to allow an animal to suffer needlessly and irreversibly, then it's not unreasonable or irrational, in my opinion, to want the same compassion and dignity for ourselves.

Deciding to forgo many months (or years) of suffering and die on one's own terms, while still able to meaningfully say goodbye to loved ones, is a deeply personal decision. In Oregon and a few other states, people with less than six months of life expectancy can legally choose assisted suicide. In those states, the decision is viewed as rational and worthy of respect within the medical and legal professions. I would like to argue that it is equally rational for someone to want to end their life on their own terms when facing severe, irreversible physical decline and suffering, even without a clear terminal diagnosis.

Of course, lots of people commit suicide without legal or medical assistance. And the vast majority of those suicides involve individuals whose despair and circumstances are far from irreversible. But that still leaves the type of assisted and dignified death I'm discussing in this opinion piece.

No one wants to end his or her life in years of pointless suffering. However, you get what you get, and what we get varies greatly. I'm in my late 70s and have lived a good, full life. I'm in very good health, and my life is still good, full, and meaningful. I'm blessed in many ways and definitely not feeling suicidal.

Yet if the time comes when I can see I'm irreversibly losing my ability to live independently and enjoy life, I would rather end it with dignity and without prolonged and pointless suffering. While the legal and ethical issues around assisted suicide are substantial, they're not insurmountable, in my opinion.

The insurance industry has its own way of dealing with suicide as a cause of death, which I believe has practical implications for medical end-of-life care. Life insurance policies pay when the insured passes away. However, for obvious reasons, they exclude paying benefits if the insured commits suicide soon after purchasing the policy. My Universal Life policy specifies a two-year exclusionary period for suicide. After two or more years have elapsed, it pays the specified benefit just as it would for any other cause of death.

The insurance industry is in business to make a profit. If it were common for suicidal individuals to purchase life insurance and then commit suicide shortly after the exclusion period, insurance companies would lose money, and they would either stop covering such cases or greatly expand the exclusionary window. The fact that my policy will pay the full benefit after a two-year exclusionary period shows that this time frame is usually enough to prevent insurance companies from giving policies to people who are already planning to take their own lives. In my opinion, the medical/legal fields could adopt a similar approach.

I believe adults should be able to submit a legal directive specifying their desire for assisted suicide under clearly defined circumstances, which would become legally actionable after a minimum of two or more years waiting period. That way, people like myself could have peace of mind knowing that, once the exclusionary window has passed and specific criteria are met, they won't have to suffer needlessly, die an undignified death, or bankrupt their families for that matter. Instead, they could legally obtain the correct prescription to first sedate, and then to end life.

It's not perfect, and certainly not for everyone, but I believe it could address many of the legal and ethical objections a person requesting to die might raise. And of course, such directives would be non-binding. People would be able to rescind, ignore, or revise their choices at any time, if they so choose.

If done properly, and with an initial exclusionary window, I believe it could reasonably eliminate concerns about giving a green light for suicide to those whose despair and wishes are transitory, and whose condition is not dire or irreversible.

Such a directive can also spare loved ones the emotional burden and trauma of watching helplessly as someone they care deeply about suffers and irreversibly deteriorates in front of their eyes, sometimes for years. It's cruel, and it's not uncommon.

In my opinion, advance directives can and should be developed with legal, ethical, and medical oversight that allows non-suicidal adults to specify their **future** wishes regarding their own end-of-life care and choices, including the option for assisted suicide, even without a clear terminal diagnosis.

In 2016, Canada passed legislation allowing people to request assisted suicide. In 2021, this law was expanded (with additional safeguards) to include those suffering without a clear terminal diagnosis. It has since become a well-received alternative to prolonged and pointless suffering. Medical Assistance in Dying (MAID) now accounts for almost 5% of all deaths in Canada. I believe that the United States could adopt similar legislation, giving people greater autonomy and dignity in how they face death. My hope is that an expanded advance directive, as I'm advocating here, can help bring that reality closer.

I feel so strongly about individuals having the freedom to make decisions about their own lives and bodies (including whether or not to have an abortion, I must add) that I wanted to end my book with this. I know my views are not for everyone... but what is?

References

American Psychological Association (2010) Social Awareness + Emotional Skills = Successful Kids, Monitor on Psychology, Vol. 41, No.4.

Bandura, A. (1977). *Social learning theory*. Englewood Cliffs, NJ: Prentice-Hall.

Binder, E.F., Yarasheski, K.E.,Steger-May, K., et al. (2005) Effects of progressive resistance training on body composition in frail older adults: results of a randomized, controlled trial. Journal of Gerontology, Nov; 60 (11), 1425-1431.

Fiatarone, M.A., O'Neill, E.F., Ryan, N.D., et al. (1994) Exercise training and nutritional supplementation for physical frailty in very elderly people. New England Journal of Medicine, June 23; 330(25), 1769-1775.

Goleman, D. (1995) Emotional Intelligence. Bantam Books.

Gottman, J., & Silver, N. (1999). *The seven principles for making marriage work*. New York, NY: Three Rivers Press.

Lutz, R., Pasick, R., Pelletier, K., & Klehr, N. (1990). *Aged to perfection: Your guide to healthy aging.* University of California School of Medicine San Francisco for the California Department of Mental Health: Office of Prevention.

Oregon Health Authority. (2022). *Death with Dignity Act requirements.* Retrieved from https://public.health.oregon.gov/ProviderPartnerResources/EvaluationResearch/DeathwithDignityAct/Pages/ors.aspx

Pascal, B. (1670). *Pensees.* Retrieved from https://en.wikipedia.org/wiki/Pensees

Pelletier, K., & Lutz, R. (1988). Healthy People – Healthy Business: A Critical Review of Stress Management Programs in the Workplace. *American Journal of Health Promotion*, 2, 5–19.

Rowe, J.W., and Kahn, R.L. (1987) Human Aging: usual and successful. Science, 143-149.

Selye, H. (1956). *The stress of life.* New York, NY: McGraw-Hill.

Selye, H. (1974). *Stress without distress.* New York, NY: J. B. Lippincott.

Wolpe, J. (1958). *Psychotherapy by reciprocal inhibition* (pp. 53–62). Stanford, CA: Stanford University Press.

Yerkes, R., & Dodson, J. (1908). The relation of strength of stimulus to rapidity of habit formation. *Journal of Comparative and Neurological Psychology*, 18, 459–482.

www.ingramcontent.com/pod-product-compliance
Lightning Source LLC
Chambersburg PA
CBHW071715120626
46550CB00001B/249